Graham R. White Christmas 1994.

A GAS STREET TRAIL

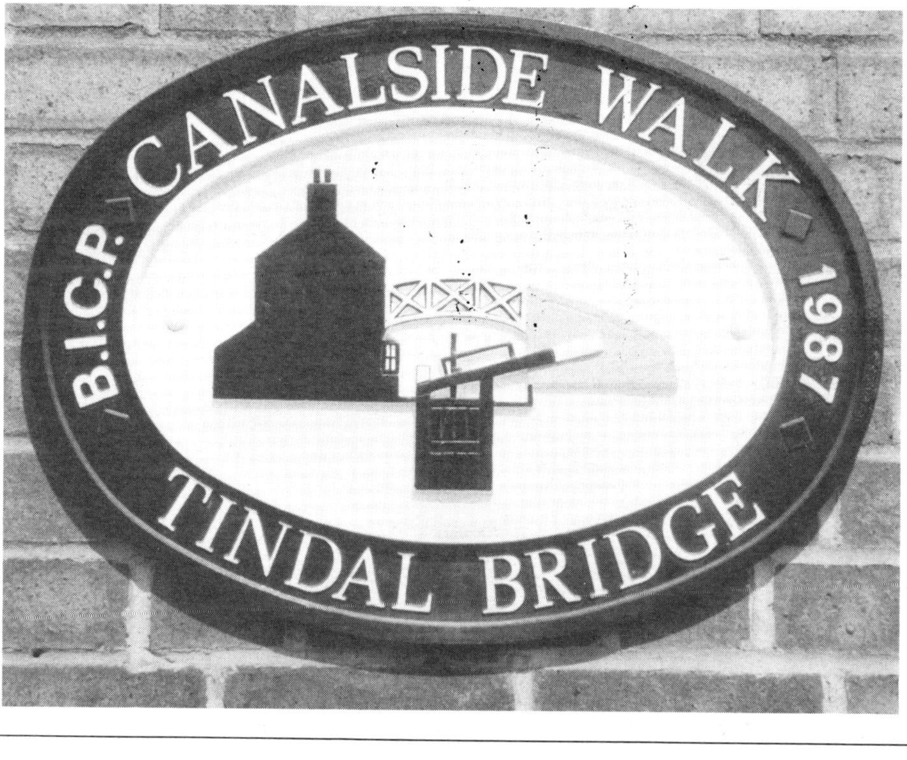

Copyright Heartland Press 1994

Shill R

A Gas Street Trail
No 1 in Local History Transport Trails

1 Canal - England - West Midlands - History
2 West Midlands - Industries - History

1 Title II Series

ISBN 0 9517755 3 7

Printed by Three Spires Print and Design
426 Bromford Lane
Washwood Heath
Birmingham B8 2RX

A

GAS STREET

TRAIL

By

Ray Shill

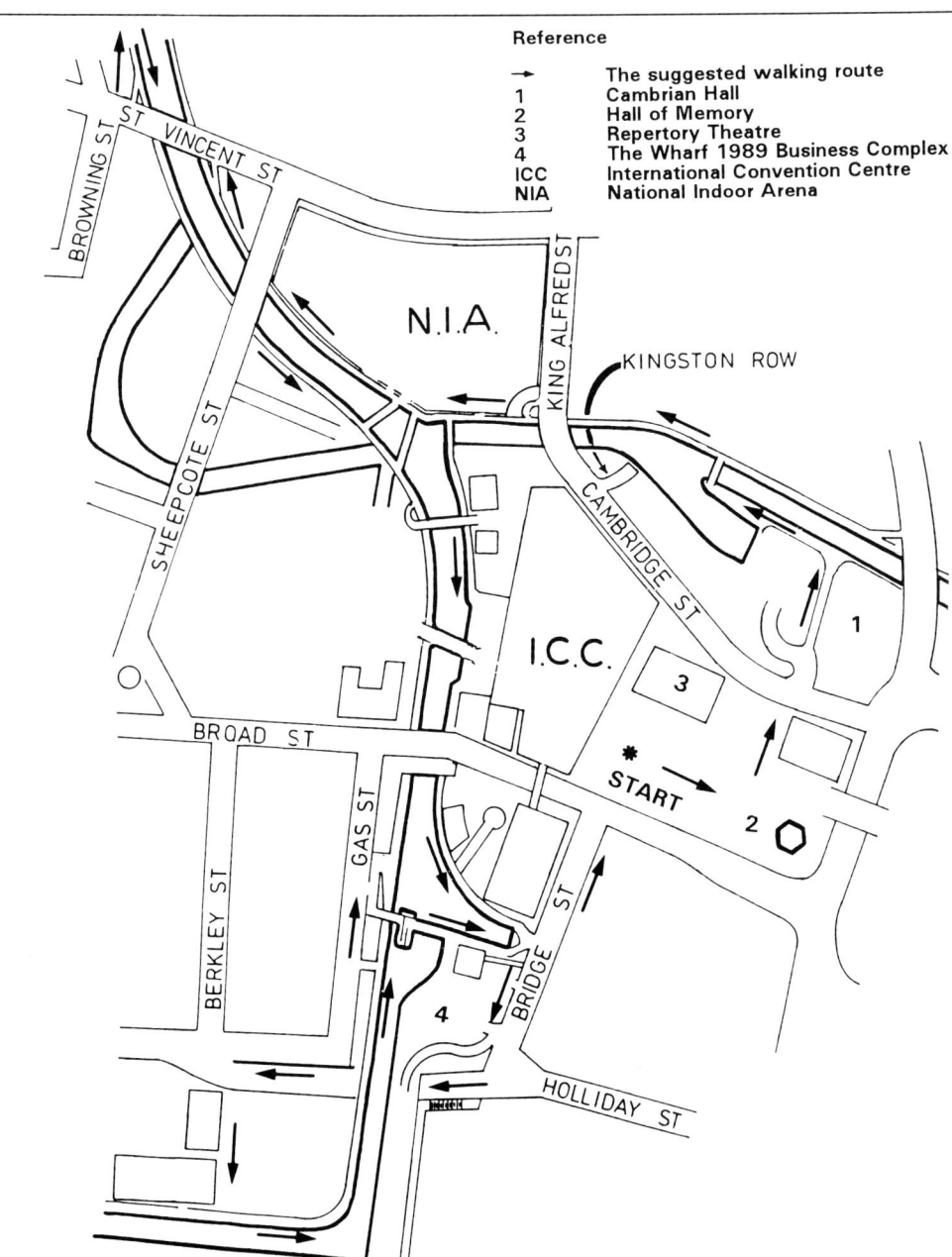

THE GAS STREET TRAIL

A walk along the canal towpaths of Birmingham.

CONTENTS

INTRODUCTION

Birmingham is recognized as a city of many trades. It is a reputation that was gained during the nineteenth century when the town of Birmingham grew into a city.

Towards the end of the eighteenth century new ideas and inventions had brought Industry out of the dark ages. Birmingham became a centre for the new industries that developed. The demand for cheap material led to a need to improve transport.

The roads were poor and the cost of taking goods by road was relatively expensive. However, a new form of transport had come into existence. It was called the canal.

Man made waterways, or canals, had existed for centuries. But these had only been built where the ground was relatively level. James Brindley demonstrated that a waterway could be made across land that was not when he built the first part of the Bridgewater Canal from the Worsley coal mines into Manchester.

Other canal schemes followed and a new transport network came into being. Birmingham was linked to growing network in 1772 and gradually canals came to serve the town's every need.

Birmingham might even be considered as an inland port, at least by nineteenth century standards. Aston Junction, The Crescent, Fazeley Street and Worcester Wharf were important transhipment areas where extensive warehouses existed.

This trail is canal orientated. It intends to show the canal heritage, particularly at Gas Street, and explain the history behind some of the surviving features. Most of the industry has now vanished, but there are still a few old buildings to be seen.

It is also important to note how the area has changed in recent years. A lot of time and money has been spent in improving the canal banks and making the towpath pleasant. Many new buildings have been constructed which include the Convention Centre and National Indoor Arena.

The whole trail can be accomplished in 90 minutes, but it is worth taking the time to explore some of the features along the route. Holliday Wharf deserves a visit, if only to look at the craft stalls and the antique shops. The towering entrance hall which separates the International Convention Centre from the Symphony Hall is also of interest. Note the fig trees which grow there.

This is a historical trail. Care has been taken to explain the walk in sections so that specific features can be discussed. It also makes the trail flexible. The reader does not have to adhere rigidly to the suggested route.

Much of the material in this book is gleaned from archive sources. The idea grew out of another project entitled the Industrial Canal which deals with the trade and traffic on the Birmingham Canal Navigations. That book is still at the research stage, but some of the material discovered was included in the Gas Street Trail.

As much original information has been included as is possible. I hope the reader finds the book as interesting as I did writing it.

Ray Shill

30/05/1994

The Hall of Memory by night.

Centenary Square

Centenary Square is the symbol of Birmingham in the 1990's. This vast open space is surrounded by buildings of consequence which are the lifeblood of the city.

It is an area which has seen considerable change within the last sixty years. The grime of industry has given way to commerce, while concrete and flowers have replaced the bricks and the soot. All is now bright where it was once grey and dingy.

At one end of the square are two imposing structures, the International Convention Centre and the Birmingham Repertory Theatre. This is where the walk commences.

Centenary Square was completed at the same time as the ICC and formed an integral part of that scheme. It was a link in a chain of improvements to the top of Broad Street which had been started in 1925 when the Hall of Memory was built.

By 1920 this part of Broad Street comprised mainly warehouses and factories. Some were dilapidated, most were grimy and dirty. Birmingham Corporation, instituted a new scheme which would transform the area occupied by these warehouses and factories. It was to be called the Civic Centre. From 1926, the council started to buy land around Broad Street as preliminary to starting the venture.

A bold scheme, the Civic Centre would have re-shaped the heart of Birmingham. There was to be a new City Hall, Public Library, a Lord Mayor's Mansion and Municipal Offices. A competition was arranged for the best design and architects from all over the world were given a chance to compete.

Maximilian Romanoff, an architect from Paris, provided the winning contribution which netted him a £1000 prize. However, even though his design was accepted, it was not acted on, the cost for such a venture eventually proved too great. Had Birmingham Corporation used his designs, the top of Broad Street and many of the associated street would have disappeared in the new development.

Birmingham Corporation were determined to proceed with the Civic Centre despite the set-back. Fresh ideas were considered and a second scheme took shape during the early 1930's. Meanwhile the Corporation continued purchase property and demolish the buildings standing there.

Limited for cash, the Corporation decided to build the Municipal Offices first. Another competition was organised in 1935, but this time it was only eligible to British architects. The best design was accepted from T.C.Howitt of Nottingham.

Construction started in 1938 and the offices were finished during 1940. When completed the building was occupied by the Government and was not handed back to the Corporation until after the War. Although only part of the intended scheme, the new building was known as the Civic Centre. Later, it was re-named Baskerville House.

After 1945 the Civic Centre concept was revitalised. A third and ambitious scheme came into being. Exhibition halls, a Civic Theatre, a Philharmonic Hall and a Hall of Marriage were included in the new proposals put forward in 1958. Little was done, however.

Eventually some of the properties taken by the Council were put to other purposes. Land which had been taken from the Birmingham Canal in Suffolk Street was used for the Alpha Tower and Television Studios.

The Philharmonic Hall should have been built in King Alfred's Place. It was never constructed, but the land was used for the New Repertory Theatre. It was constructed 1969-1971 and replaced the *Old* theatre in Station Street.

By 1986 it seemed that the Civic Centre was dead and buried, yet the Council still wanted to improve the area. They had high hopes to host the Olympic Games. A new scheme came into being which involved a Convention Centre, a Symphonic Hall and an Indoor Arena.

The fourth building program began in 1986 and met with considerably more success than the previous schemes. It took five years to complete, but the top of Broad Street was finally transformed with the construction of the Hyatt Regency Hotel, the International Convention Centre and the National Indoor Area.

Sixty-seven years have elapsed since Birmingham had started the Broad Street improvement, but work still goes on. In 1993 work on Brindley Place commenced. When completed this new development will create new leisure facilities in Cumberland and Oozells Street.

The Birmingham Repertory Theatre as it first appeared in 1973. Bingley Hall is just visible on the extreme left of the picture.

Baskerville House was originally known as the Civic Centre after the scheme responsible for the construction. Had this proposal been completed there would have been identical building where the ICC now stands.

From Centenary Square to Brindley Walk

Centenary Square - Hall of Memory - Baskerville House - Cambridge Street - Brindley Drive - Cambrian Hall- Brindley Walk.

Centenary Square fills the space between two former streets; Baskerville Place and King Alfred's Place. The site had been occupied for many years by Thomas Messenger and his factory which produced chandeliers and ornamental brass-work. Messenger's works were demolished as part of the 1935 Civic Centre scheme.

The ICC stands on several old properties including the entire Bingley Estate which once occupied all the land between King Edward's Place and King Alfred's Place. At first there was a large house, Bingley House, and grounds which belonged to the Charles Lloyd.

In 1849 the house and grounds were host to Birmingham's first trade exhibition. Bingley House was pulled down shortly afterwards and in its place Bingley Hall was erected. This Hall was to become a major exhibition centre and held all types of shows until the early 1980's

Next to Bingley Hall, and also on the Bingley Estate, was the Prince of Wales Theatre. This theatre had opened in 1856 as the Birmingham Music Hall and after various changes of title became the Prince of Wales Theatre in 1865. A wide range of productions including operas, play and pantomimes were performed and the theatre enjoyed a good deal of success with *top* names often on attendance.

In April 1941 a German bomb scored a direct hit on the theatre completely destroying the interior. No attempt was made to repair it and afterwards the site passed to other uses. All traces of the building were removed in 1987 during excavation work for the ICC.

History has a strange way of repeating itself, however. The new Symphony Hall which forms part of the ICC complex occupies the site of the old Prince of Wales Theatre.

We cross Centenary Square to the Hall of Memory. A strip of grass in front of the Hall provides a reminder of the gardens laid out there in 1925 when the Hall of Memory was opened .

The Hall replaced older buildings established between 1810 and 1840. Every piece of ground was crammed with some form of industry. A screw factory owned by Guest Keen and Nettlefold stood on the corner of Baskerville Place. Next to them was Thomas Bolton's rolling mills which faced Broad Street. Other premises included timber yards, coal and limestone wharves.

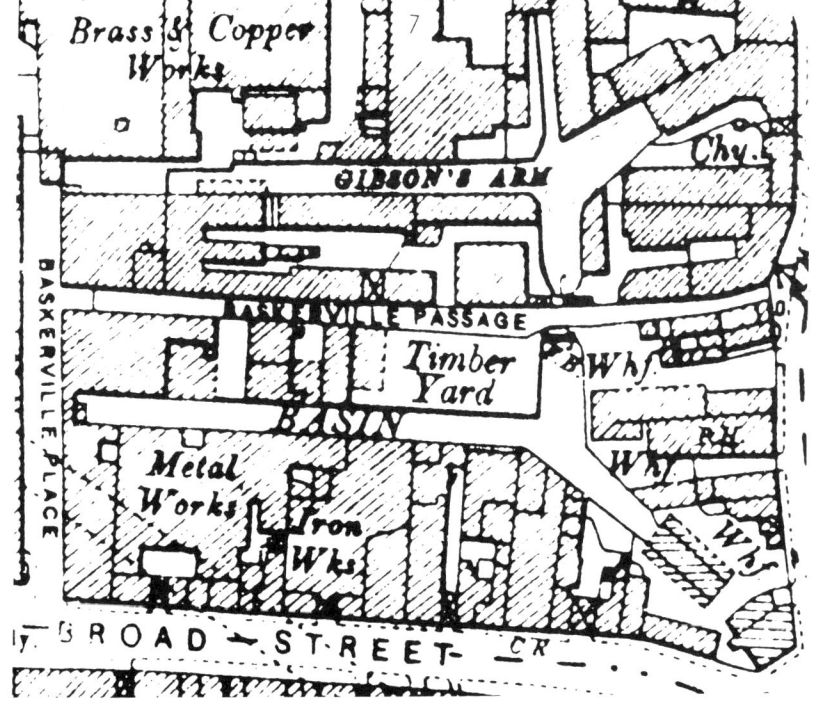

The Baskerville Canal basins as reproduced from Ordnance Survey Map, surveyed 1902. R.W Winfield's Brass & Copper Works occupied the top left, while Thomas Bolton's Metal and Ironworks are noted bottom left. The Public House which faced Easy Row was known as the Queen's Arms

There was a colonnade constructed along the length of old Baskerville Place which faced the gardens. A row of benches were arranged inside so that people might sit and relax or reflect. These gardens were a popular meeting place for office workers seeking a lunchtime break and wedding parties lining up to have photographs taken. When work started on making Centenary Square, the colonnade was taken down brick by brick and re-erected beside St Thomas's Church.

The Hall was built to commemorate those who had died in the First World War and remains a monument to all who have perished through conflict.

It is a small but impressive building, octagonal in shape built of Portland stone on a base of Cornish granite. Large brass doors stand under a portico which leads to inner doors also of bronze. Four bronze statues stand on granite pedestals. They represent the Air Force, Army, Navy and Women's service.

Baskerville House is another impressive building. The house is named after John Baskerville who lived here 1745-1775. John Baskerville earned a fortune making japanware and used his money to establish a book printing business.

The printing works were located on his estate, which was then known as Easy Hill. From the press came a range of fine quality books which included the classics and religious works. Through his books Baskerville raised Birmingham to the status of an important publishing and literary centre.

There is a small sculpture which stands in front of Baskerville House which comprises the letters LIGRIV. It commemorates John Baskerville's first book, an edition of Virgil, published in 1757.

Birmingham has honoured John Baskerville in many ways in the past; a place, a passage and a street have all preserved his name. There also was another Baskerville House which was used as Court House during the middle of the nineteenth century. This building stood on the corner of Easy Row and Broad Street, but was removed when Broad Street was widened in 1925.

John Baskerville died in 1775 and much of his property at Easy Hill passed to the Ryland family and then Thomas Gibson.

Gibson built a mill beside Cambridge Street and in 1812 constructed a private canal to link the works with the Newhall branch of the Birmingham Canal Navigation.

Gibson's Canal was built at a higher level than the Birmingham Canal to which it was linked. It passed under Cambridge Street to a deep lock which raised the boats up to the arm. Water was pumped into the basins with the aid of a steam engine located in a pump house beside the lock. Thomas Gibson derived a revenue from all boats which navigated his canal.

The canal served two long basins arranged in the shape of a letter F and collectively they were known as the Baskerville Basins. At the top of the F was Broad Street where Thomas Bolton's mill and William Bolton's timber yard existed. The second basin, known specifically as Gibson's Arm served the mill and foundry erected by Gibson and later worked by a variety of proprietors. It also served R.W. Winfield's Rolling Mills. The Gibson branch once carried considerable traffic to these separate establishments.

Winfield's were noted for their ornamental brass work and in particular brass bedsteads. Their goods were made to a high standard and won medals at trade exhibitions for their work.

The rolling mills were established in 1824 by a group of Birmingham businessmen which included Robert Winfield, brass founder. It was a business which prospered and grew. Other property was purchased on both sides of Gibson's Arm. By 1897 there was an extensive plant on the site which comprised rolling, wire drawing and brass tube drawing mills.

ON THE CANAL IN BIRMINGHAM   A.Morrow

These works were a hive of activity as men toiled in all parts of the factory bent on every different aspects of brass work. Strip casting, wire drawing and lacquering were performed in different departments situated around the canal basin. Long rooms were filled with brass bedsteads, brass chandeliers and all sorts of ecclesiastical brass and gilt work. A labyrinth of stairs and wooden galleries ran through the works and spilled over the canal below as rickety walk-ways.

Transport to and within the works involved the canal, but there were no towpaths for the horses to drag the boats. The brute strength of the boatman was the only means by which craft could navigate these waterways. Boats were propelled by a technique known as shafting where the boatman pushed a long pole against the bottom to force his craft along.

The canal was in perpetual shade because of the tall buildings which lined the waterway. Boats glided through the inky black water with cargoes of coal and metal for the mills. It was a dark gloomy place reminiscent of some of Charles Dickens novels.

From 1853 Robert Winfield had sole charge of the works and was responsible for much of the firms original expansion. They eventually became responsible for the pump house and lock and gained any revenue from boats passing through to other works. In 1897 Winfield Ltd called in the receiver and they were then purchased by Dugard & Mitchell who traded as Winfield Rolling Mills Ltd.

The basins nearest Broad Street were filled in during the 1920's so that the Hall of Memory and adjacent gardens could be built. Gibson's basin which served Winfield's works lasted longer. As late as 1934 Leonard Leigh brought coal from Brownhills to their factory. Winfield's finally closed in 1936 and the site was purchased by Birmingham Corporation.

An aerial view of the top of Broad Street about 1931. Winfield's works are to be seen in the lower centre of the picture. Gibson's Lock and basin are clearly shown beside these works. Other features include: the Hall of Memory (centre), Messenger's premises (bottom right), Broad Street Corner (upper centre) and the site of the Old Wharf which had been filled in and was then in use as car park (upper right).

Courtesy Birmingham Library Archives.

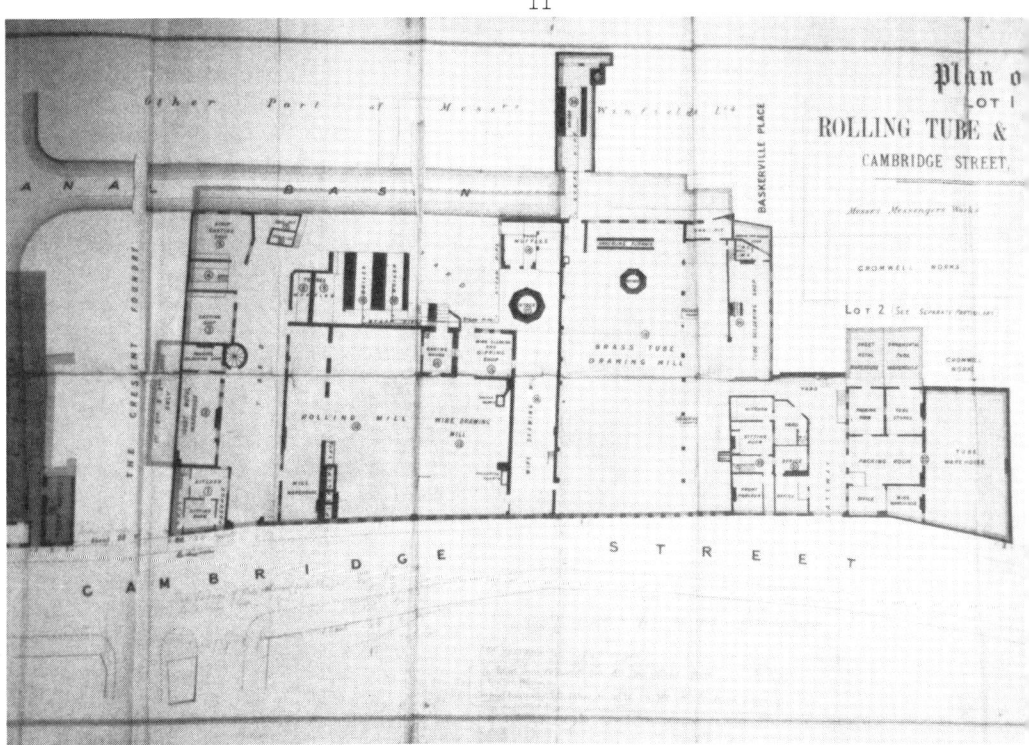

Winfield's Rolling Mill in Cambridge Street from a plan of 1897. Winfield's were noted for their ornamental brass work and in particular brass bedsteads. By 1897 they had an extensive plant which included rolling, wire drawing and brass tube drawing mills. They also had charge of the two storey pump house, the lock and any revenue derived from passing boats. *Courtesy Birmingham Library Archives.*

R. W. WINFIELD,
Patentee & Manufacturer of
BRASS & IRON BEDSTEADS
& General Brass Founder,
No. 141 Fleet Street, LONDON,
& Cambridge St. Works, BIRMINGHAM.

Brass, Copper, Iron, Tin and Cased Tubing.
Plain and Ornamental Gas Fittings.
Railings, Cornice Poles, Ends, Rings and Brackets.
Patent and other Castors, Stair Rods &c. &c.

An advertisement from Wrightsons 1847 Directory of Birmingham.

All traces of Gibson's lock were removed in 1938 when the foundations for Baskerville House were excavated. It is however still possible to follow a similar route to that which the Gibson's Arm took from the Newhall Branch.

This can be done by following the path beside Baskerville House to Cambridge Street which is crossed to reach to Brindley Drive. A footpath in front of Cambrian Hall leads to Brindley Walk.

The course of Gibson's canal passed through the grounds of Cambrian Hall to join the Birmingham Canal. Buildings mostly covered the waterway so that it ran in a virtual tunnel from the lock to the Newhall Branch. Near the junction the waterway widened into a basin which had wharves on both sides. These served the Cambridge Street Timber Yard and one of the merchandise carrier depots on Crescent Wharf.

Brindley Drive and Walk are named after James Brindley, the canal engineer, who was responsible for the construction of many early canals. The Birmingham Canal was but one of his projects.

It was built at the request of a number of prominent Birmingham citizens who became shareholders and proprietors of the Canal Company. These included eminent people such as Matthew Boulton, Dr John Ash and Samuel Galton.

The Birmingham Canal joined the Staffordshire & Worcestershire Canal at Autherley. When it was completed in 1772, goods could be sent from Birmingham to the ports of Bristol, Liverpool and Hull by water.

Merchandise traffic was , however, only a part of the goods consigned by the canal, the bulk was coal. The main purpose of the Birmingham Canal was to bring coal from the collieries around Bilston, Tipton and West Bromwich into the heart of Birmingham.

Coal was an important commodity. It literally fuelled the fires of Birmingham's industry and any reduction in the cost was beneficial to the firms then operating in the town. Coal had been previously carried by waggon and cart along poor roads and was expensive to buy. The canal reduced the cost of transport considerably. People now paid half than what they had paid before. It was no small wonder, therefore, that when the first boat load was unloaded in November 1769, the bells were said to have rung out throughout Birmingham.

A view of the Farmers Bridge Locks as they pass under Summer Row at Saturday Bridge. There are 13 locks in the flight which raises the level of the canal 81 ft.

From Brindley Walk to the National Indoor Arena

Brindley Walk - Farmers Bridge Junction - Roving Bridge over Canal - Old Toll House - Tindall Street Bridge - National Indoor Arena.

Brindley Walk was opened in 1969 and follows the course of the Newhall Branch Canal. Our trail reaches Brindley Walk at the point where steps lead down to a lower level. It is worth pausing here to survey the scene.

On one side of the fence is the Birmingham & Fazeley Canal which descends through at series of 13 locks from Farmers Bridge to Snow Hill. The line of the canal can be seen to cut a straight path between tall buildings until its lost in their shadow.

The Architects made use of a natural dip in the land when designing Brindley Walk and at the same time restored an old right of way. At this spot the old Dudley Turnpike meandered behind the back of John Baskerville's home and printing works. During the early 1770's a new road, Summer Row, was cut which straightened the route into Birmingham and left this part of the turnpike as a simple trail.

Brindley's canal reached this location in 1769 and a temporary wharf was constructed near the old Dudley Turnpike. Coal brought from mines near West Bromwich was unloaded here and then carted into the town.

During 1769 a dispute had developed concerning the final terminus of the Birmingham Canal. According to James Brindley's plan the canal should have ended at Newhall Ring, the residence of the Colmore family, but another scheme had been put forward by the canal company which considered a piece of land in Brick Kiln Croft as a more suitable terminus.

Charles Colmore was determined that the canal should end on his land and engaged in a bitter dispute with the canal proprietors. He successfully had an Act of Parliament passed to compel the Birmingham Canal to complete their canal to Newhall Ring.

The Birmingham Canal Company were equally determined to make their terminus in Brick-Kiln Croft. Eventually both lines of canal were built. They became known, respectively, as the Newhall and the Paradise Street Branches.

Charles Colmore's route was finished first, even though the canal proprietors put several obstacles in the way of its completion. An aqueduct was constructed to carry the canal over the old turnpike. The canal then passed under Friday Street and followed a course parallel to Great Charles Street before terminating at Newhall Ring.

The piece of property known as Newhall Ring was converted into Newhall Street and other roads such as Lionel Street were quickly established nearby. New buildings sprang up on both side of the canal as businessmen sought to establish water-borne commerce. The Colmore estate was later to obtain a considerable revenue from these properties.

Several wharves were made on the side of the canal which faced Great Charles Street. One of the first merchandise carriers to use the Birmingham Canal was Hugh Henshall. He took one of Great Charles Street wharves in 1777. Henshall was followed shortly afterwards by another carrier Gilbert and Worthington who leased an adjacent piece of land.

The Birmingham Coal Company established a wharf at the end of the Newhall Branch during 1793. It was their hope to reduce the price of coal which according to their articles *had been very much advanced in price but also had become very scarce*. The Coal Company was formed to *purchase and work mines of coal vending the same in Birmingham*. Many local people had shares in this company which cost ten shilling each to buy. They later purchased land at Toll End near Tipton and developed coal and ironworks there. Coal and iron was brought by canal to their Newhall Street warehouses.

Other works located near the end of the branch included the Lionel Street Foundry and the Albion Flour Mill, both had frontages in Lionel Street.

Friday Street was renamed Congreve Street, but the bridge over the Newhall Branch continued to be called Friday Bridge. A wharf was established beside this bridge and opposite Great Charles Street. A number of carriers used this wharf until about 1850.

Although freight composed much of the canal trade, some passengers were carried. Passenger boats, or Packets as they were generally known, started to appear on British canals about 1800.

There was a packet boat terminus at Friday Bridge which is mentioned in trade directories for 1800 and 1801. How long it lasted is unknown, but during the 1820's another packet was started by a Tipton boat builder, Thomas Monk. The boat, known as the Euphrates Packet, operated from Tipton to Friday Bridge and completed the journey in two hours.

Monk later extended his service to Wolverhampton. In 1843 the packet boat was taken over by the Swift Packet Company. Using sleek boats and fast teams of horses, the Swift Packet was able to reduce the journey from Birmingham to Wolverhampton to two hours. The Swift Packet ceased running in 1852 and the boats were sold.

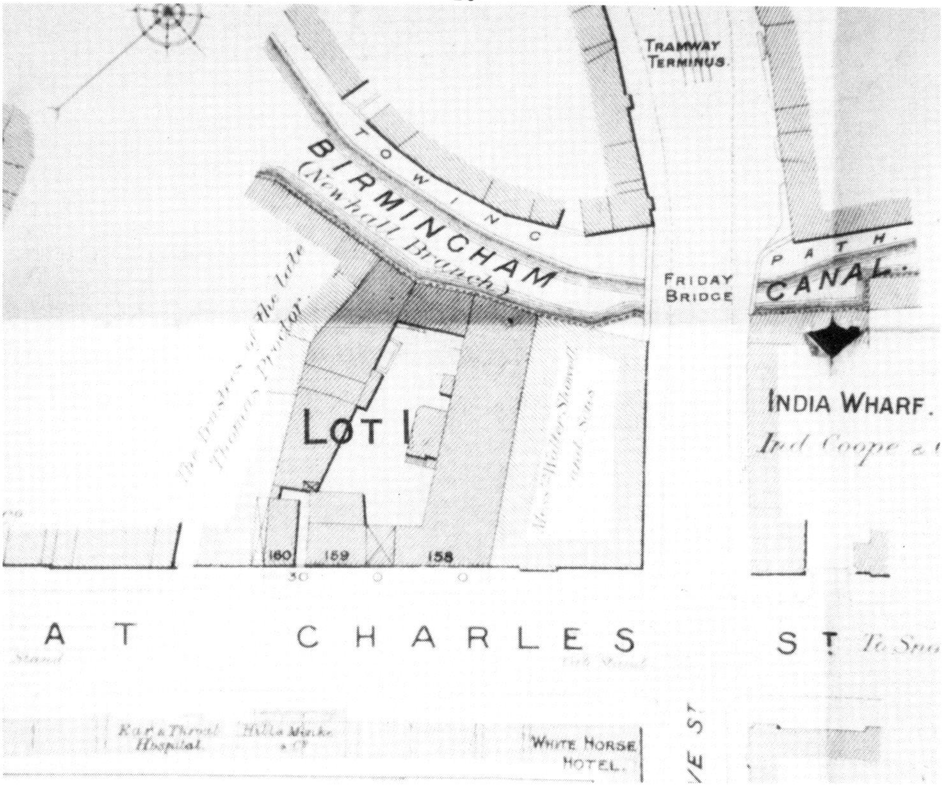

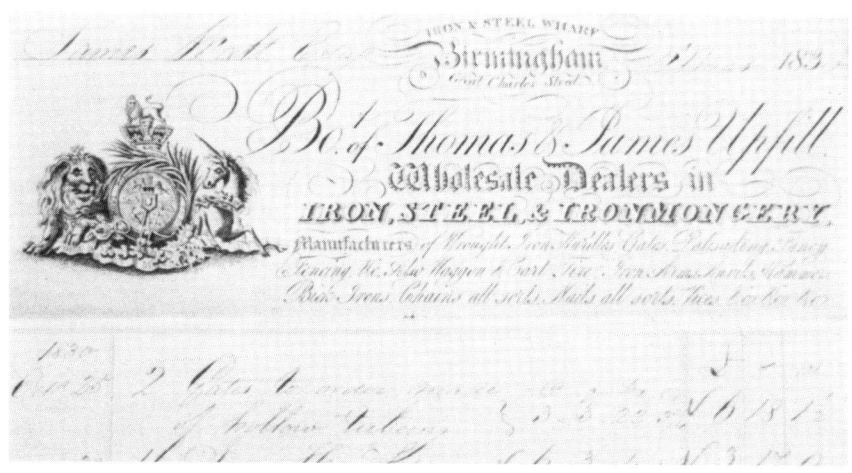

A plan which shows Friday Bridge and the location of the Ind Coope wharf c1900
Courtesy Birmingham Library Archives.

A bill head for Thomas Uphill who is an example of the many firms who had wharves
beside the Newhall Branch Canal   *Courtesy Birmingham Library Archives*

In later years, brewers Ind Coope and Walter Showell established wharves on the Newhall Branch. Ind Coope brought beer from their brewery in Burton, while Showell carried beer in their own boats from the Crosswell's Brewery at Langley Green.

Timber was also carried along the Newhall Branch and several timber yards were established near its banks. The first was made near Friday Bridge by John Iddins on land he had leased from the Colmore family.

The timber trade continued long after Iddins death. During the 1850's Fountleroy & Sons had a timber yard at 161 Great Charles Street. A basin which joined the Newhall Branch served both this timber yard and Crockett's coal wharf.

About 1937 the Newhall Street end of the canal was bought by Birmingham Corporation as part of their Civic Centre scheme. It was their intention to take other land later. The section was closed off and drained.

Our walk continues along Brindley Walk towards Farmer's Bridge. We follow the route of the old towpath which ran on this side of the canal. On the opposite side of the walk (and the old canal) where the grass now grows once stood numerous warehouses which were known as the Crescent Wharves.

The original name for these wharves was Farmer's Wharf which is derived from the local landowner James Farmer. The wharf was located beside an occupation bridge which crossed the canal, which became known as Farmer's Bridge.

James Farmer was a Quaker. Normally quakers abhor violence, but surprisingly James was a successful gun maker. He had gone into partnership with his son-in-law, Samuel Galton who carried on the business after Farmers death in 1773.

Farmer's Wharf was developed during 1789 as a lime wharf. In 1789 May and Norton had built lime kilns nearby. Limestone was brought from Dudley by boat to the kilns and burnt to make lime. At this time, lime was important to the building industry because it was a basic ingredient of mortar. There was thus a steady, if not increasing, demand for the substance.

Gradually other wharves were made along the line of the canal towards Friday Bridge. At the end of July 1791, Thomas Russell & Co erected a temporary warehouse on Farmers Wharf. Russell & Co were dealers and general merchandise carriers from Stourport. They became the first carriers to establish a depot at this place. Rock and Company also established a coal wharf here in 1791.

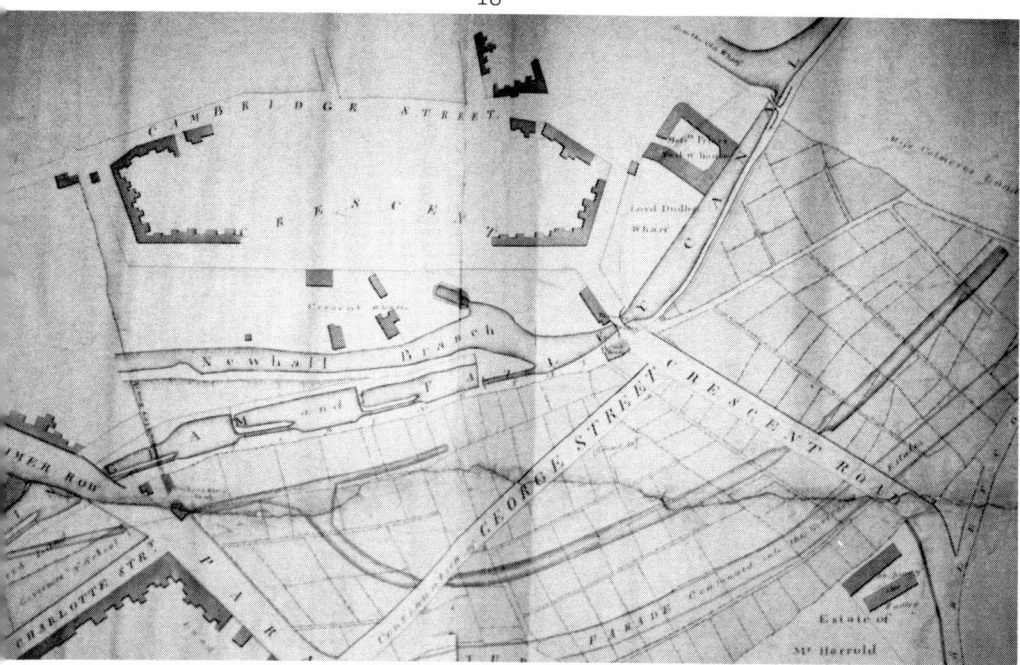

An 1809 plan which show the canal, street and wharves around the Crescent. It also shows an intended canal from the Birmingham & Fazeley Canal to the Sandpits, which was not built. Lord Dudley's Wharf and Mr Price's warehouse are also shown.

Courtesy Birmingham Library Archives Ref:478656.

A plan of John Whitehouse & Son's wharf at the Crescent which appears on lease dated 24 June 1827 *Lee Crowder Collection, Birmingham Public Library.*

Cambrian Wharf and the top of Farmer's Bridge Locks as they were prior to 1960. Several warehouses and wharves line the waterway. This once was a busy scene with boats clustered around both sides of the canal. The warehouses formerly used by Picton and Fellows, Morton & Clayton & Co can be seen in the centre of the picture.

Courtesy Birmingham Public Library.

A view of Cambrian Wharf from the rear. The road which ran from Kingston Row behind Crescent Wharf is seen in the foreground, while the Crescent follows the high ground on the right of the Picture. The Flapper and Firkin Public House now occupies the space taken by Falk's premises.

Courtesy Birmingham Public Library.

Charles Norton, who owned the lime wharf, was responsible for the construction of an elegant row of houses built on a new road which lay between the canal and Cambridge Street. In a short time these buildings, the street in which they were situated and the wharves they faced became known as the Crescent.

The Crescent was actually built on a terrace raised above the canal wharves. Another road ran along the perimeter of this terrace but at lower level to serve the canal-side properties.

These wharves were once a busy place. Before the railways came into existence, several important carriers had depots at the Crescent. They include names such as Thomas Sherratt, John Whitehouse & Sons, George Ryder Bird, Nathan & German Wheatcroft and Crowley & Hicklin.

By 1840 there were five separate establishments on the Crescent where the boats unloaded their goods. Each had its own little army of porters to load, unload or consign goods to the warehouse. In some cases an agent was in charge of the depot. Often he would be assisted by a number of clerks. In other cases where the carriers were a family concern a member of that family took charge. For example William Whitehouse was responsible for the business conducted by John Whitehouse and Sons, while George Ryder Bird Junior looked after his fathers trade.

Many of these carriers disappeared after the railways were established but others took their place. Some of the wharves were now used by other firms. Harper & Moore, firebrick manufacturers of Cradley, had a pot yard here by 1848.

Two big carriers depots developed at either end of the Crescent. At No 1 Crescent Wharf, which faced the Gibson Arm, the Shropshire Union Railway & Canal Company enlarged the buildings formerly used by Thomas Sturland.

There was a large, three storied, warehouse block which ran from the Gibson Arm to the wharf road. At the end which faced the wharf road was a general office. In front of the warehouse was a shippers office which faced the wharf. There was also a small stable block for three horses which stood alongside the wharf road. About 1893, the premises were further enlarged when agent's and clerk's offices were built on the land between the stables and the general office.

At the other end of the Crescent (No.5 & No.6 wharves) was Crowley's depot. They were important canal carriers who had established a wharf here by 1807. Crowley and Co later became railway carriers, but kept their Crescent Wharf site for a number of years. The Shropshire Union later took over these premises and made improvements to them during the mid 1880's.

Little remains of the Newhall Branch, but what little is left is used for boat moorings.

The top of Farmers Bridge Locks and Cambrian Wharf as they appear today. The skyline is very different to what it was in 1960.

The last carrier to use the Crescent Wharves was Fellows, Morton and Clayton, who had taken two wharves from the Shropshire Union Canal Carrying Company when they ceased trading in 1921. They used them until 1949 and thereafter the old carriers wharves saw little use.

The only piece of the Newhall Canal to remain is the arm opposite the Flapper & Firkin. This part became known as Cambrian Wharf from about 1880 onwards. It is, in fact, the oldest part the Crescent Wharves and the remains of old vaults are still to be seen beside this public house.

When Brindley Walk was made, Cambrian Wharf was re-built at the same time. A new public house was constructed at the waters edge which became the Longboat. The decor inside the Longboat was canal orientated and some of the furniture represented parts of boats. It was popular with boaters who often moored alongside. In the autumn of 1993 the pub closed for re-fitting and re-opened as the new Flapper & Firkin. The cobbled way down to the public house is all that is left of the old wharf road.

Cambrian Wharf continued to be used for handling limestone well into the twentieth century. Norton and Williams had them until the end of the nineteenth century. Subsequent owners of these wharves were Charles Nelson, the Stockton limestone quarry owners.

Walter Showell also had a distribution depot here for a number of years. Barrels of beer brought from their brewery were once a common waterside sight.

At Farmer's Bridge Junction there is plaque on the hovel which suggests the Birmingham & Fazeley Canal had been completed to this junction in 1783. This date actually refers to the Act of Parliament which authorised the construction of the canal. Another four years would pass before the Fazeley canal would be made to this point.

The Act of Parliament and canal company records refer to the bridge as *Mrs* Farmer's Bridge. The lady in question was Priscilla Farmer, wife of the late James Farmer previously mentioned.

The Birmingham & Fazeley Canal began as a rival scheme to the old Birmingham Canal. The original scheme proposed a new canal from Fazeley to Wednesbury with a branch into the lower part of Birmingham at Digbeth. Supporters of the idea saw it providing a shorter route for Wednesbury coal to reach London. The Birmingham Canal naturally opposed the Fazeley Canal.

Eventually a compromise was reached whereby the route of the canal was diverted via Birmingham to join the Newhall Branch at Mrs Farmer's Bridge. The Fazeley Company had the use of the old canal as far as West Bromwich to reach the other, disjointed, part of their line to Wednesbury.

A year after the Act had been passed granting the Birmingham and Fazeley Company the right to build their canal, the two canal companies merged. For the next ten years, the combined venture was known by the rather long-winded title; the Birmingham and Birmingham and Fazeley Canal.

The Farmer's Bridge flight of locks were completed in stages by the contractor Thomas Sheasby. By Monday 5th November 1787 the stretch from Farmers Bridge to Church Street had been finished and filled with water.

A roving bridge is still in place which enabled the barge horses to cross the Fazeley line to reach the Newhall Branch. We cross this bridge and descend by the toll house.

Most canal traffic paid tolls in one way or another and it was necessary to have such houses at strategic places, so that the traffic could be accurately charged. In this fashion the canal company derived its revenue.

The tolls varied according to distance and type of traffic. Some carriers received special rates and the toll clerks had to keep books and distance tables to charge correctly.

At Farmer's Bridge the toll house has recently been re-built. The old building was accidently demolished whilst construction work went on behind it. Most the buildings which line the towpath at this location are of recent build. On the right hand side of the new 'old' toll office was a boatman's mission, but this disappeared many years ago.

The Farmer's Bridge flight of locks handled an enormous amount of traffic. Gas lamps were even installed so that boats could navigate the locks during the long winter nights.

In the days before this innovation, boats were only allowed to operate during certain hours. At night Farmer's Bridge Junction was often crammed with canal craft waiting to go down.

James Deykin was a carrier who evidently chose to load his fly boats with as much merchandise as they could carry. On the 22nd January 1811 one of Deykin's vessels left the Crescent Wharf for London.

Her captain was Edward Southward. He brought the boat to the top of Farmer's Bridge Locks where the canal was already congested with boats waiting for the morning. Southwood moored his boat in the middle of the canal next to three others; one was owned by the Wolverhampton Boat Company, the other two belonged to William Judd. Edward then went home to Smethwick for a nights rest and left the vessel in the hands of two helpers. He returned the next morning to find the boat sunk.

The Toll Office at the top of Farmer's Bridge Locks was once very busy. It was manned continuously as boats navigated this canal at all times of the day and night. Gas lamps were provided along the flight to aid the boatmen.

In recent years the towpath has been improved and new buildings have been erected along the canal at Farmers Bridge. One unplanned reconstruction was the Toll House which was accidently demolished and had to be re-built.

Kingston Buildings were once a nail warehouse owned by Thomas Price. There are still mooring rings in the brickwork where boats tied up alongside.

During the night some water had been drawn out of the canal so that maintenance work could be undertaken. Deykin's boat had settled to the bottom and the weight of the cargo had broken her back. The unfortunate carriers now had a thousand pounds worth of cargo irretrievably lost and two hundred pounds worth of damage done to their vessel!

A few yards further along the towpath are two BCN canal houses. They are readily identifiable as such because they bear iron number plates. The BCN numbered many of their buildings and the characteristic plates are still carried on surviving buildings.

On the opposite side of the canal is Kingston Row and the remains of the site where James Farmer's bridge crossed the waterway. Some of the houses in Kingston Row also carry BCN number plates as evidence of one time canal ownership.

The path across Farmer's Bridge eventually became a street which led to Crescent Road. This bridge was taken down during the 1820's and the canal widened at this point. At the same time a new road was made across the canal from Cambridge Street which became King Edward's Road. The new bridge was called Tindal Bridge.

Lord Dudley had a wharf beside the canal between Farmer's Bridge and Tindal Bridge. This old wharf lies behind the Kingston Row cottages and is presently used as a mooring by the Birmingham & Midland Canal Carrying Co Ltd.

Beyond Tindal Bridge is an old canal-side property known as Kingston Buildings. In 1809 this was Price's Nail Warehouse. Nails were produced in vast numbers in different parts of the Black Country and especially in Dudley and Tipton. No doubt there was traffic along the canal to this warehouse. In later years Kingston Buildings were occupied by various merchants. The old iron rings which still remain in the wall provide evidence of the canal boats which must have moored alongside.

On the towpath side was a timber yard and a long timber wharf. As late as 1970 tall piles of timber could be seen stacked there. After a period of dereliction the site was taken for the new National Indoor Arena. This building was completed in 1991 now provides a venue for a wide range of sporting events.

The NIA occupies a large piece of land and the building line follows the towpath from Tindal Bridge to Sherborne Street. Part of the Arena is constructed upon the site of Monument Lane locomotive shed. Another piece spans the Birmingham and Wolverhampton railway.

An evening view of the canal cottages at the top of Farmers Bridge Locks in 1983. Farmer's Bridge crossed in the centre of the picture.

Kingston Buildings and Tindal Bridge. Kingston Wharf was situated on the right of the photograph.

From The National Indoor Arena to St Vincent Street

National Indoor Arena - Old Turn Junction - Sheepcote Street Bridge - St Vincent Street Bridge

This part of the walk starts from the point where four lines of canal meet. Until recently this junction was known as Farmer's Bridge. As mentioned earlier, this was a name which had been originally given to the junction with the Newhall Branch at the top of the locks. When that branch closed the name was transferred to here.

The new title was only used for about thirty years. In 1993 the name changed again, it was re-christened Old Turn Junction.

It was, in fact, the fourth change of name for this particular canal junction and also a change back to a previous title. The first name given to it was Deep Cutting Junction.

When the waterway was made only two branches of the canal, the Newhall and Paradise Street, met at this point. The line to Paradise Street passed through a steep sided cutting and so the name Deep Cutting Junction came into being.

The name Old Turn originates from the fact that in 1825 the canal at this point was altered. A new line was cut through land which then belonged to Caroline Colmore to shorten the route of a stretch of the *old* Birmingham Canal.

To confuse matters both titles were used at the same time. It seems that it was BCN practice to use two names at double junctions with respect to what was classed as the *main* line. Those vessels which took the Old Birmingham Canal towards Oozells Street traversed what was Old Turn Junction, whilst those which went towards Gas Street went across Deep Cutting Junction.

The line of the Old Canal as made to Brindley's specifications followed the contours of the land and on the approach to Birmingham wound and curved at frequent intervals. As it passed through Ladywood the original line came almost as far as Sheepcote Street before turning west. The canal then passed through the Oozells Estate, which belonged to the Colmore Family, and then carried on towards Newhall Ring.

The new line was completed under the direction of Thomas Telford and was the start of an extensive scheme to shorten the main line to Wolverhampton.

Improvements to Brindley's original canal had been going on since 1800. Odd pieces of canal had been widened and some of the kinks taken out of the route. A more serious alteration was contemplated in 1821 when a new canal was proposed from Sandy Turn to Deep

A train comes out of the tunnel and passes the site of Monument Lane Engine Sheds. The National Indoor Arena now covers the entire site.

An 1978 view of Old Turn Junction. The sign post on the traffic island was different to the one that presently stands there.

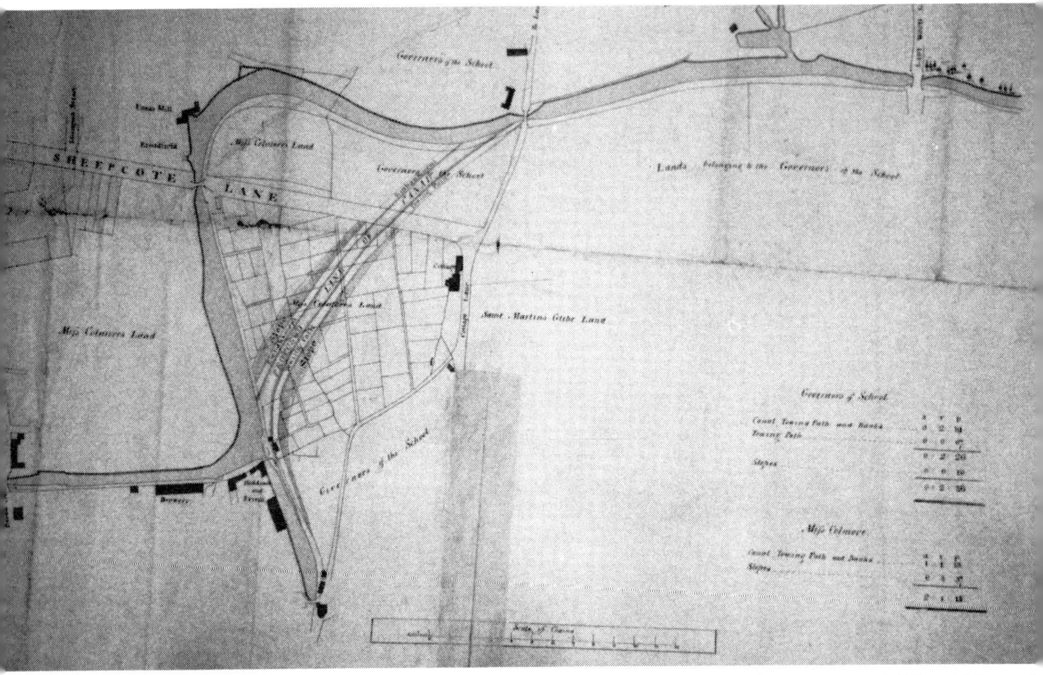

Plan dated 1821 of the proposed canal across the lands of Miss Colmore and King Edward V1 Grammar School to join Sandy Turn with Deep Cutting Junction. This scheme, which had a single towpath, was modified by Telford in 1825. *Courtesy Birmingham Reference Library (Archives Dept.)*

The former Public Works Department Stone Wharf in Sheepcote Street.

Cutting Junction across the lands of Miss Colmore. While negotiations went on to acquire the property a more general scheme concerning the whole canal was developed.

An original plan shows that a single towpath was intended for the short piece to Sandy Turn. When Telford was appointed engineer he modified the plan to include a towpath on either side.

There are two Horseley Company roving bridges at the junction which were built shortly after these alterations were carried out. One spans the canal towards Farmer's Bridge, the other crosses Telford's main line. Another BCN bridge completes the link across the line of the Old Birmingham Canal. In 1993 a fourth bridge was constructed across the junction to link the Indoor Arena with the towpath on the other side.

We continue along the towpath towards Sheepcote Street with the vast NIA building on the right. The towpath edge is lined with long stone blocks laid down to Telford's specification. In some parts the edging has been replaced with modern blue bricks where repairs have been done. On the opposite bank, near Sheepcote Street Bridge, there is a long section of blue brick where a basin once was located to serve Grice & Grice's Tubeworks.

The Grice family had two works, one at Nile Street and another at Heath Street South. Both faced the canal, although latterly most of their traffic was handled by the railway companies. They made copper and brass tubes for the railway and shipping industries. Their Nile Street works took water out of the canal for cooling purposes. In 1918, they signed agreement with the BCN to take 9,944,000 gallons per year.

After Sheepcote Street Bridge has been passed the style of the buildings changes from the modern to victorian. We pass on the right the Corporation Stone Wharf and Highway's Depot. The distinctive circular buildings now stand idle awaiting a purchaser or re-development.

The Old Birmingham Canal joins the Telford's route from the left at Ladywood Junction. This junction was previously known as Sandy Turn Junction. The name *Sandy Turn* originated from a particularly tight curve at this place where boats frequently stuck. About 1800 the kink was smoothed out, but boats continued to ground here until Telford's improvements.

When St Vincent Street is reached, we follow the path up onto the road and cross the canal. A better view can be obtained of the Corporation Stone Wharf from this bridge.

The other towpath is now taken as we descend the ramp from the end of St Vincent Street Bridge. Telford's canal continues towards Ladywood. Our route follows this towpath back into town.

From St Vincent Street to Old Turn Junction

St Vincent Street - Sheepcote Street - Old Turn Junction

A row of modern homes line the towpath on the far side of the canal. These have been built on the site of the Monument Lane railway coal depot. In the foreground is the remains of an old basin where the towpath edge is concreted over. This marks the basin which served the Midland Flour Mills. Fellows Morton and Clayton carried grain and flour for them to different parts of the country.

Soon after passing under St Vincent Street Bridge, the towpath rises to pass over a section of the Old Birmingham Canal called the Oozells Canal Loop. Until the autumn of 1993 many boats lined the banks of the Oozells Loop. Most were hire boats which were based at the Alvechurch Boat Centre, Sherborne Street Wharf. Their depot has now closed and the future of the wharf is uncertain.

Sherborne Street Wharf has a complicated history. It began as a wharf which served Lovekin's boat yard. Later a long basin was cut from the old main line to Baker's Paper Mills and then under Sherborne Street towards Ryland Street. Sherborne Street Wharf was built alongside this basin and was home to a few coal merchants. In 1938 the site was taken by Fellows Morton and Clayton who enlarged the wharf and built new offices and warehouses. It is upon the former Fellows, Morton & Clayton site that the Alvechuch Boat Centre now stands.

The large black building is the last surviving canal warehouse in this area and the most modern. It was built for Fellows, Morton & Clayton when it was decided to demolish their Crescent warehouses as part of the Civic Centre scheme. The building comprises three floors; a basement, ground floor and first floor. At the front is a large canopy which extends over the canal to provide shelter for the boats unloading and loading below, while at the rear is a bay for the motor vehicles.

Other warehouses were planned but not built. In 1949, the wharf and warehouse passed to the Docks and Inland Waterways Executive and was used for a number of years particularly for metal traffic.

The warehouse occupies the site of an early flour mill. This was known as the New Union Mill and was built in 1813 on land leased from Miss Colmore. The mill, like many of its time, was owned by a joint stock company and was established to provide cheap bread.

Between the Mill and Sheepcote Street was Broadfield's Dock. Thomas Broadfield established a boat building yard here on land leased from Caroline Colmore in 1808. This dock is mentioned in several early advertisements concerning the sale and re-sale of canal craft. Thomas died in 1826 and the boat yard closed.

Ladywood Junction once better known as Sandy Turn Junction marks the place where the old line (Oozells Loop) diverges from the main canal.

Boats belonging to the Alvechurch Boat Centre are lined up under the canopy of the former Fellows, Morton & Clayton Warehouse.

Above A boat is moored alongside the Alvechurch Boat Centre wharf, Sherborne Street in July 1993.

Left Sherborne Street Wharf c1947. A Fellows, Morton & Clayton vessel is moored beside the wharf. *Courtesy Birmingham Reference Library (Archives Dept.)*

The original course of the canal from Deep Cutting Junction to Sandy Turn.

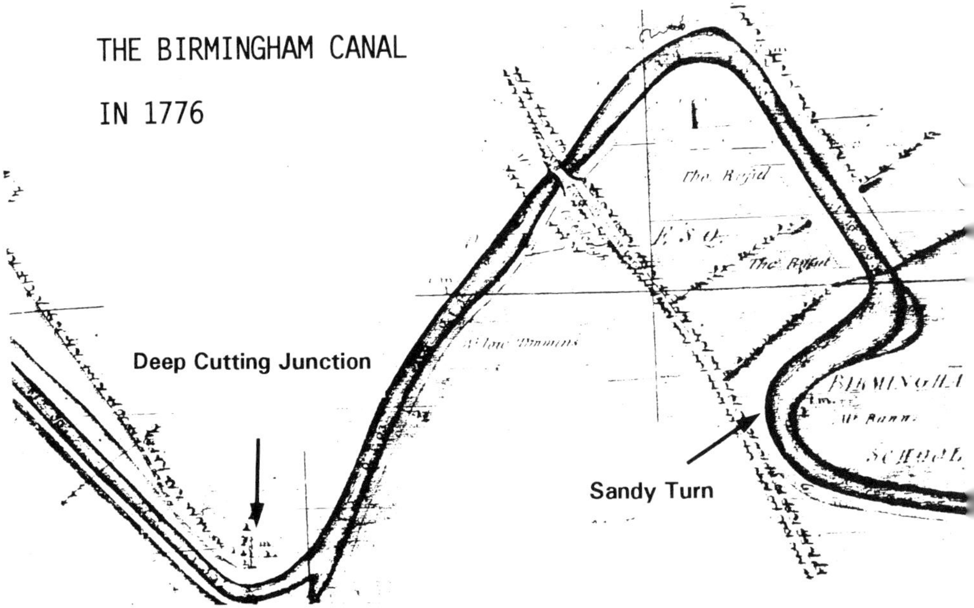

THE BIRMINGHAM CANAL

IN 1776

Deep Cutting Junction

Sandy Turn

Map of the Old Line near Tindal Street as reproduced from the Ordnance Survey printed in 1888. Wharves to note include (A) Ladywood Dock, (B) Winfield's Coal Wharf, (C) Jones & Fitzmaurice Stone Wharf and (D) Sherborne Wharf.

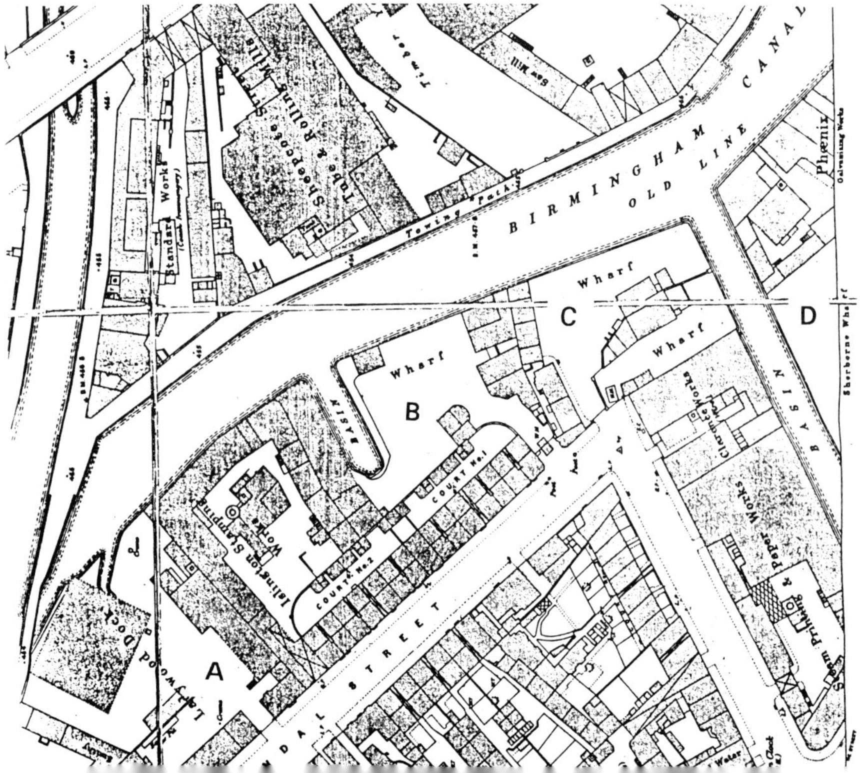

There were other wharves and basin which have now disappeared. They include Winfield's coal wharf and Jones & Fitzmaurice's stone wharf. Some served other boat yards. One owned by the Carter family stood near Ladywood Junction on Browning Street, and was known as Ladywood Dock. Carter's boat-yard was involved with several boat building syndicates or societies during its long life.

Canal boats were expensive items to buy and to ease the burden people would join a boat society and pay for the boat they had, or wanted, in instalments. It was particularly common amongst coal merchants to do this since they often lacked the funds to buy a boat outright.

The Birmingham Boat Company No.3 established in 1858, was one which used Carter's yard. For boat builders such as John Carter the society provided a source revenue at lean times. In 1874 the Ladywood Dock and Carter's other boatyard in Aston was acquired by the Birmingham & Midland Boat Building Co Ltd. John Carter and his son, also John, were principal shareholders.

Beyond Sheepcote Street Bridge there is a fine view of the Birmingham skyline. The Hyatt Regency Hotel, Alpha Tower and the British Telecom Tower are all readily noticeable.

Returning to Old Turn Junction one part of the towpath rises to cross by a Horseley Company bridge. When the ramp is climbed a better view can be obtained of the other half of the Oozells Loop towards Sheepcote Street.

At the time of writing most of the property on this side of the canal has been demolished. It is proposed to build new houses and a leisure development as part of the Brindley Place Scheme.

The scene before us looks very different to what it was when the canals were crowded with vessels. On the left hand side of the waterway were the extensive Oozells Coal Wharves. They were busy wharves where boats laden with coal from Cannock Chase unloaded for the coal merchants located there.

On the right hand side were located brick wharves. George Wood had a wharf near Old Turn Junction where bricks and tiles were brought by boat from his Oldbury brickyard for sale in Birmingham. Another brickmaker, George and James Brawn had a yard close to the old Sheepcote Street canal bridge

In between these two brick wharves was the Albion Tube Works. These works had been built in 1858 for George Stacey, but he had died before the sale had been completed. They were finally purchased in 1859 by Edward and Samuel Lloyd who trade as Lloyd & LLoyd for a number of years at this site. The Albion Tube Works eventually became part of the Stewarts and Lloyds empire. As late as 1928, tubes were sent here from Coombswood Tube Works by canal boat.

These buildings are referred to as the Old Union Mill, although they were part of the New Union Mill. The first Union Mill, in Birmingham, was located in Holt Street.

Sheepcote Street Bridge frames the Birmingham skyline. The Hyatt Regency Hotel and the Alpha Tower are both visible in this shot.

The Albion site has now being razed to the ground, but the remains of Nile Street can still be seen to cross the site. Nile Street was originally a public street which served the tube works, the brick wharves and BCN wharf near Old Turn Junction.

LLOYD AND LLOYD,

ALBION TUBE WORKS,

NILE ST., BIRMINGHAM,

MANUFACTURERS OF

PATENT LAP-WELDED IRON TUBES,

FOR LOCOMOTIVE, MARINE, AND STATIONARY BOILERS;

Also, Manufacturers of

IMPROVED HOMOGENEOUS METAL TUBES

AND ALL DESCRIPTIONS OF

Tubes and Fittings for Gas, Steam and Water, Plain, Galvanized and Enamelled.

GUN-METAL STEAM GLAND COCKS, WATER GAUGES, &c.,

Of very Superior Manufacture, supplied on the Shortest Notice.

An advertisement published in the 1860 Birmingham Directory.

HORSELEY IRON WORKS
STAFFORDSHIRE
1827

The Horseley Company were located at Tipton. They made a number of bridges for different canal companies.

A view of Farmer's Bridge (Old Turn) Junction before the new bridge was placed across the junction.

From Old Turn Junction to Bridge Street

Old Turn Junction - Brewery Basin - The Energy Centre -The International Convention Centre - Broad Street Bridge - The Glassworks - Bridge Street.

There is choice of recommended routes offered for this stage of the walk. There are number of bridges which pass over the canal, but not all may be available for public use at any one time. It is suggested that the reader crosses the two Horseley Roving Bridges to the other side of the canal, but British Waterways may close these for essential repairs at any time. If this happens the reader is advised to use the next available bridge.

Each Horseley bridge bears the date 1827 which signifies the year they were erected. The first was a new bridge built to cater for the new towpath arrangements. The second, which spans the branch to Farmer's Bridge, replaced an earlier (*brick* ?) bridge of 1773 vintage constructed when the canal was opened to Brick Kiln Croft.

On the other side the towpath remains raised above canal level so as to pass over a brick bridge, built about 1815, to span a basin made to serve the Birmingham Brewery. This basin has now been filled in, but the bridge has survived.

The Birmingham Brewery was owned by a joint stock company which was formed in 1814. Beer was brewed on the site for a number of years under the name of the Birmingham Brewery Company. Brewing ceased about 1881, but the maltings were continued for a number of years by Henry Mitchell.

Just beyond Brewery Basin is a tall brick building with distinctive metal chimneys. This is the Energy Centre and provides the power for the vast NIA/ICC complex. The sharp-eyed might notice the small portraits of Telford and Smeaton built into the wall. Few find, however, Brindley's portrait hidden high up on the other side of the building.

When the branch to Paradise Street was first contemplated, it was the ideas of the planners to construct part of the canal in a tunnel. That idea was eventually dropped and the canal was made through a deep cutting to the Hagley Turnpike.

The steep embankment were later replaced by brick on both sides of the canal. On this side it was to accommodate a new street called St Peters Place which derives its name from a Roman Catholic Chapel.

Until 1780 it was unlawful to hold a Roman Catholic mass in this country. When the chapel was built in 1783 the church authorities thought it prudent for the exterior of the building to disguised as factory so as to escape notice.

The Second City trip boat Europa passes under the new bridge at Farmer's Bridge Junction.

A portion of the a map dated 1825 which shows the canal and other features in the Broad Street area.

Courtesy Birmingham Library Archives

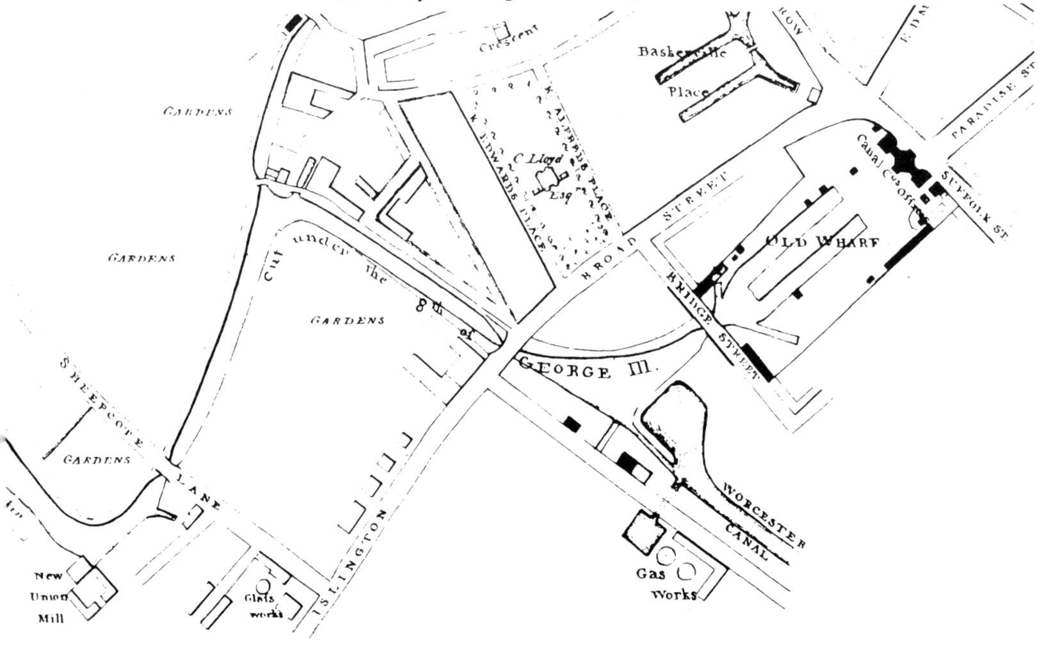

Two trip boats line up alongside the ICC ready to take people on tours of the local canals. This particular view has now been obstructed through the construction of a bridge over the canal to the Waters Edge development.

St Peters Place followed the canal towards the Birmingham Brewery buildings. Only the Brewmaster's house now survives. It stands above the canal next to a bridge which crosses the canal. The rest of St Peters Place was swept away when the ICC was constructed.

On the other side of the Brewmaster's house is one of the main entrances to the ICC. The dark facade of glass rises above the small square which meets the towpath. In front of this entrance is the rather unusual foundation stone which stands apart from the main building. It was laid in 1986 by Jacques Delors when he was President of the European Commission.

A wharf has been made here for the tour boats which now take people on guided trips along the local canal network. It is worth taking a ride on one of these boats if only to see the canal side features from water level.

Until the end of 1993 there was an un-obstructed view of the trip boats from the opposite towpath. In January 1994, a new bridge was erected over the wharf to the new Waters Edge development now under construction.

The Waters Edge, when completed, will be a collection of canal-side shops, cafes and restaurants. At the time of publication, work on the main buildings is well advanced.

Next to Waters Edge is the Brasshouse, which faces Broad Street. The original brasshouse was built by the Birmingham Metal Company in 1780 to provide cheaper brass to the town than hitherto had been obtained from Bristol. Other brassworks superseded it and by 1835 had become a warehouse occupied by Thomas Pemberton. In 1874 the building was converted into a Waterworks Office and latterly saw use as a weights and measures office before being re-built as a public house and restaurant.

Broad Street has a complicated history. It first formed part of the Hagley turnpike from Easy Row to the Brasshouse. Beyond the Brasshouse and as far as Five Ways, the road was known as Islington. By 1840 the whole street as far as Five Ways was called Broad Street, but there remained separate numbering sequences; one for Broad Street (Islington) and the other for Broad Street (Easy Row). The canal became the dividing line between the two. During the 1870's one numbering system was finally adopted for the whole street.

In 1858 a group of trustees belonging to the Unitarian Church, purchased a two strips of the towpath near Broad Street Bridge. It was their intention to build a new place of worship, the Church of the Messiah, over the canal next to the Brasshouse.

Branson & Gwthyer were responsible for the building work which was completed in November 1861. The dedication service for the new church took place on the 1st January 1862. A Sunday School was also built over the canal behind the church.

There once was a roving bridge beside Broad Street which crossed the canal, but this was covered by the Church of the Messiah. Another replaced it, but at a place closer to Old Turn Junction.

A set of steps lead up to Broad Street and the Crown Inn. The Crown is an old Birmingham pub which has been recently refurbished. It proudly bears the date 1781 which is when the first ale house was established on this site. The present structure is much more modern however. Many of the major changes happened after William Butler took over the pub in March 1890. Butler also established a brewery behind the public house. These later buildings were lost when the ICC was constructed. The Crown, however, has happily survived and its clock tower has become a canal-side feature.

Broad Street Bridge was once the site of another packet boat terminus. In 1850 John Inshaw ran a steam packet, twice a day from here to Bilston Street Bridge in Wolverhampton.

Cranes were once common waterside features. They were often found near warehouses and assisted the loading and un-loading of canal craft. This particular crane, which formerly installed at Sneyd, was placed beside the towpath below the Brasshouse a couple of years ago but was removed again when work started on Waters Edge.

A few extracts from the 1830 editions of Aris's Gazette....

18/01/1830. Baskerville Wharf. John Warden in partnership with brother in coal and coke and brick trade. Intends to carry on own account. Coals and Cokes, best Tipton Blue Bricks, Best Newcastle Blue Tiles, Blue and Red Quarries, Wilnecote Tiles and Bricks, Stourbridge Firebricks etc...

01/02/1830. To be Let and be entered upon at Lady Day next (or sooner) very extensive warehouse in Cambridge Street and abutting upon the best side of the canal which has been used as an iron and corn warehouse also wharf and wharf lands. Apply Thomas Gibson No.3 the Crescent

24/05/1830. Sale of Capital Wharf situated in Broad Street adjacent to BCN Basin with sluice and convenience for loading and unloading boats late in the occupation of Messr. Danks & Co, Carriers & Wharfingers now in the occupation of Mr Kendrick, corn dealer. Sale in includes warehouses, stabling and offices.

21/06/1830, To be sold by private contract, The BIRMINGHAM BRASSWORKS, on the banks of the Birmingham Canal in Broad Street.

Our route follows the towpath through Broad Street Tunnel. Care needs to be taken when walking under Broad Street because there is limited head room. We emerge at what is popularly known as Gas Street Basin. This large expanse of water is surrounded by buildings which are both old and new. On one side are arranged old canal cottages and former toll offices, whilst on the other are public houses, restaurants and offices erected within the last few years.

Canal boats congregate here and take berths around the basin or Worcester Bar which run across the centre. Gas Street Basin also provides moorings for people who live on the boats. A floating community has existed here since the canal went into decline. Their gaily decorated boats, which often had a working past, add to the variety of craft which use Gas Street.

Gas Street is actually the point where the Birmingham Canal meets the Worcester and Birmingham Canal. Worcester Bar marks the boundary between each canal.

Since Brewery Basin we have followed the route of the original towpath to Paradise Street. The towpath on the opposite bank was added about 1825 when Telford improved the Birmingham Canal. Both towpaths have been upgraded and replaced in the last few years with new bricks as part of the many improvements made to the canal banks in this area.

We follow the path towards Bridge Street and pass the wall of an old iron foundry. The path soon becomes a steep climb as a roving bridge is encountered. This bridge once spanned an old canal basin now reduced to an ornamental pool.

The wharves around this basin were first used by carriers. Robert Skey, John Wall and Samuel Danks had established depots here by 1795. Other merchandise traders such as James Shipton continued to use the basin until 1840.

Gradually the land fronting Broad Street was taken for other purposes and a host of firms had access to the canal and basin at different times. In addition to the iron foundry, there were Gibbs and Canning, terra-cotta manufacturers, who brought their wares from Glascote. There was also a glassworks at 295 Broad Street.

The Glassworks was owned by the Green family but in 1857 was taken by Alfred Arculus who produced a range of fine cut glass and crystal. In later years the canal basin appears to have been primarily used for the glass traffic and in BCN distance tables is referred to as the Arculus Etna Glasswork basin.

Alfred Arculus evidently had other interests and according to trade directories was described as an electroplate manufacturer. In his final years he entered politics and served as a councillor for the Market Hall Ward. He died in November 1875, aged only 51. His glass making business was carried on as Arculus & Co until 1925.

Gas Street Basin in 1979. The skyline was very different at that time. All the old warehouses had been demolished and the Post Office buildings were visible from most parts of the basin.

A collection of camping, pleasure and trip boats are noted at Gas Street in 1989.

The site of the old glassworks has been covered by the Hyatt Regency Hotel. Yet its memory has been preserved by the present Glassworks. This is a public house and restaurant which has adapted part of the old iron foundry in memory of the old Etna Glassworks.

Access to the wharf was by a public right of way from Broad Street which passed between the buildings. Every square foot of space was utilised in one way or another.

Amongst the properties which faced Broad Street were Ephraim Cutler's glass warehouse (272 Broad Street) and William Vale's Refreshment Rooms.

There once were a group of buildings which followed the towpath as far as Bridge Street. Some were almost as old as the canal and originally comprised the iron warehouses of Benjamin Stokes.

Stokes was a partner in the Coseley Ironworks at Deepfields and iron blooms were brought by boat to Stokes warehouse in Birmingham. These premises passed through a number of owners and suffered various alterations before being taken by William Pearce.

William Pearce was a merchant who dealt in glass and lead goods. Pearce had moved his business from Edmund Street for the larger premises in Bridge Street. William produced a range of decorative glass work and built up an important glass merchants business. He was later joined by Ephraim Cutler and the firm then became Pearce & Cutler.

The Birmingham Canal now finishes at Bridge Street, but when first constructed it passed onto the Old Wharf. There were two long basins here built in the shape of a tuning fork. At the far end stood the offices of the Birmingham Canal Company opened in 1773. Before this date the company had rented a smaller office in Newhall Street.

This was the main terminus for the canal trade and during its long life has been known under several names. Brick Kiln Croft was the first since this was the name given to the piece of land on which it was built. It was known as Paradise Street Wharf for a time and another name was Suffolk Street Wharf, at other times it was simply The Wharf.

A later title, and perhaps the most regularly used, was the Old Wharf. This seems to have been derived from the fact that at the start of the nineteenth century the Birmingham Canal was commonly known as the Old Birmingham Canal and the wharf quite naturally as the Old Birmingham Canal Wharf. It was not long before this name was shortened to the Old Wharf and it was this title which stuck!

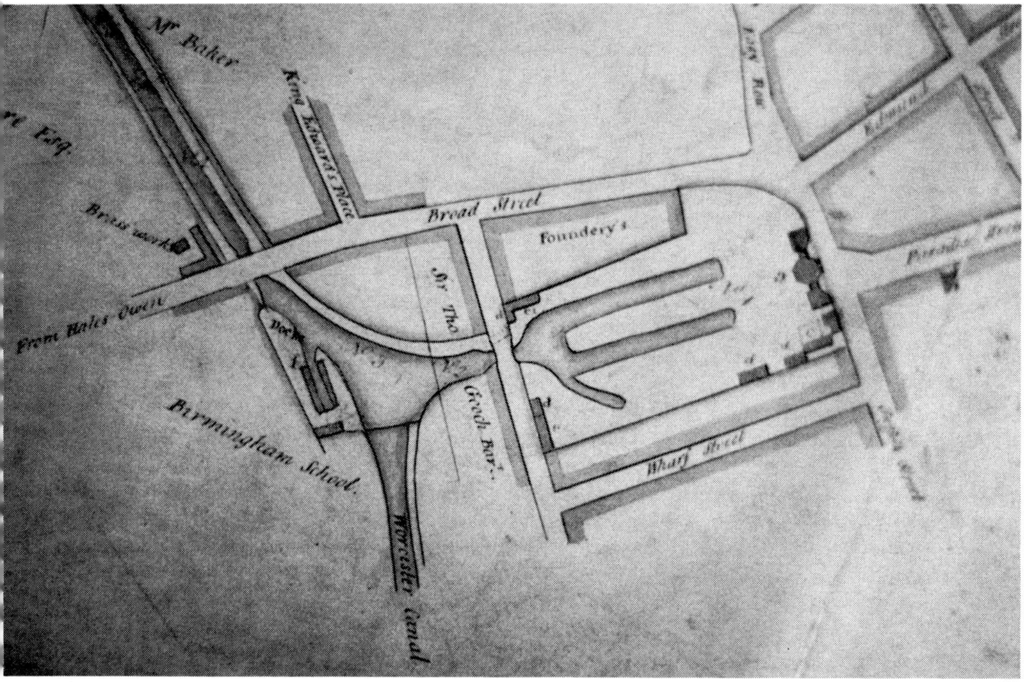

A plan of Gas Street from a map dated 1806 which shows Bird's boat building dock. *Courtesy Birmingham Reference Library (Archives Dept.)*

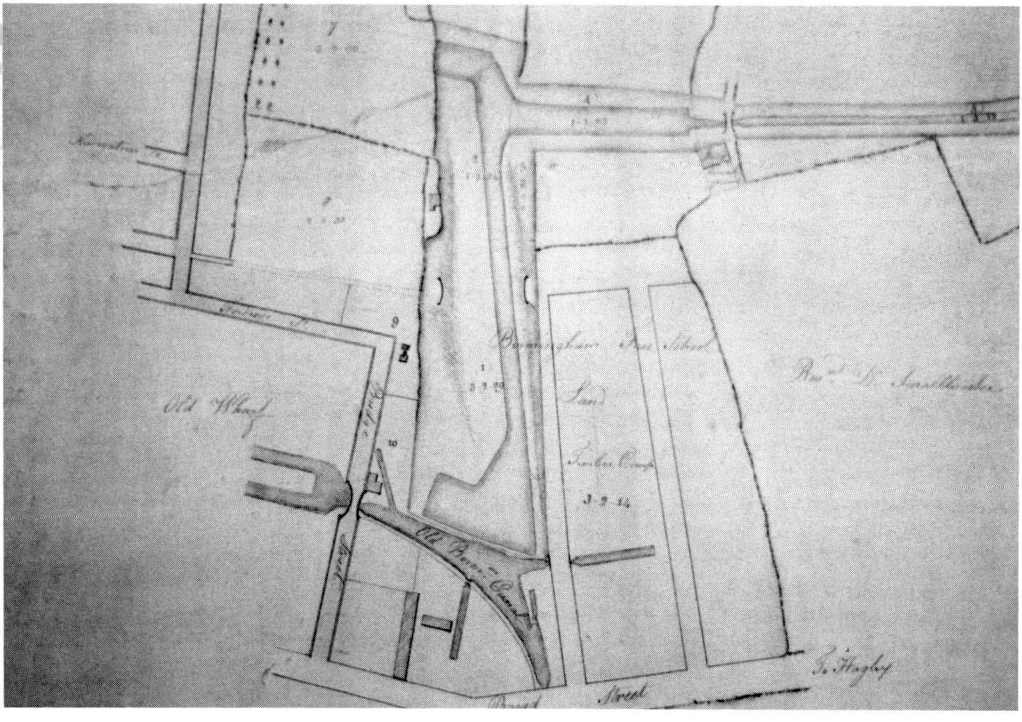

A plan of Gas Street from the Robins Collection which dates from c 1795.

Gas Street in the Snow (1). A narrow boat resident prefers a makeshift plank to cross the Bar Lock than to use the bridge.

Gas Street in the Snow (2). A fresh fall of snow completely covers the basin.

Gas Street in the Snow (3). A view along Worcester Bar.

Gas Street in the Snow (4). Sunny Valley, which formerly belonged to Samuel Barlow, is one of several boats moored at Worcester Bar.

Gas Street in the Snow (5). A view of the basin as seen from Quayside Tower.

From Bridge Street to Granville Street Bridge

Bridge Street - Holliday Street - Worcester Canal Aqueduct - Holliday Street Wharf

The walk takes us down Bridge Street to Holliday Street around the back of the old Wharves and the new development that has replaced them. Hotels, offices and apartments now stand where there was once warehouses and wharf buildings.

A public house, the James Brindley, is built on the site of old basins once used as a carriers depot and later as cement wharves. Thomas James Graham was a wharfinger here and agent to Greaves, Bull and Lakin who sent plaster and cement by boat from their quarries in Warwickshire.

The James Brindley is distinctive canal side public house built on two levels. Access to the upper floor is reached from Bridge Street, whilst the lower floor can be entered from the towpath. It is worth a visit if only to look at the local canal photographs arranged around the walls.

A little further down Bridge Street was the large Severn & Canal Carrying Company's warehouse and wharf. Here goods were transhipped into carts and later lorries for local delivery. After nationalisation this depot passed to British Waterways who used it until the mid 1960's. The buildings lay unused there-after and were pulled down in 1975.

The wharves here were the start of a range of canal side property known as the Worcester Wharf. The canal was actually built above the natural level of the land, which drops towards Holliday Street. Spoil had to be brought to this spot to make the wharf up to the level of the canal.

At the bottom of Bridge Street was one of the main entrances to Worcester Wharf. A few boatman's cottages have survived near this entrance which date from the early 1880's. A wide cobbled way led from here up to a public wharf opposite Worcester Turn.

This particular entrance way was made during the mid 1870's as part of scheme of wharf reconstruction carried out by the canal company. These alterations came about because the West Suburban Railway intended to build their line across the Wharf to a terminus in Suffolk Street. Prior to 1870 there were several gateways to different wharves and warehouses.

There was also a wharf office which was erected when the first section of Worcester & Birmingham Canal had opened. This office faced a road known as Wharf Street which joined Bridge Street with Suffolk Street. The office was demolished after 1873 when the new entrance to Worcester Wharf was made.

We turn right into Holliday Street and view the aqueduct which carries the Worcester and Birmingham Canal over the street. This aqueduct was re-built in 1885 when Holliday Street was itself enlarged and carried forward to Suffolk Street. These alterations were done at the same time as the Midland Railway built their new Central Goods Station. Norfolk St was swept away with excavation work for the new goods depot. Much of Fordrough Street and part of Bridge Street was also removed.

Holliday Street originally finished at the bottom of Gas Street and a narrow passageway known as the Gullet passed under the Worcester and Birmingham Canal and between two sides of Worcester Wharf to Fordrough Street. The Gullet and all the old buildings associated with it disappeared when Holliday Street was enlarged and deepened to pass under the canal.

In old Wharf Street there were many courts and alleyways. Six public houses were also to be found in this street, three on either side. Most were demolished when the Central Goods Station was constructed. On the corner of Bridge Street and the 'new' Holliday Street where the petrol station now stands was a Boatman's Hall and mission. The mission replaced an earlier Hall and Bethel Chapel which had stood on Worcester Wharf, but which had to be removed when the new street was constructed.

The new Boatman's Hall was completed at the end of 1884 and comprised two floors. On the ground floor was a coffee and reading room, whilst on the first floor were a classroom, mission room and a school-room for the boatmens children. Part of the cost to the construction for the new building was met by the Midland Railway.

Before 1873 one of two main entrances to Worcester Wharf was a continuation of Bridge Street. This was a road, or thoroughfare, which served the different warehouses and timber yards. It continued round the wharves and eventually joined the end of Blucher Street, which was the other entrance.

In addition to the industrial premises, a number of dwellings were placed along this road which housed a number of families. This small community comprised a varied collection of people which ranged from porters and carters associated with the warehouses to sawyers and foremen employed by the timber yards. Most of these properties were purchased by the Midland Railway and demolished to make way for the new Central Goods Station.

In order to maintain the public right of way across Worcester Wharf, a public footpath called Holliday Passage was constructed by the Midland Railway. Steps lead up the passage which runs behind the Wharf to Commercial Street.

We continue along Holliday Street and pass under the aqueduct. The structure is actually a combined covered way and aqueduct, because it supports the carriage way up to Worcester Wharf as well as the

BOATMEN'S HALL, WORCESTER WHARF.

Boatman's cottages, Worcester Wharf. This picture, of 1985, shows the situation before the wharf road was repaired.

water way. Note decorative iron roof supports and the white glazed tiles laid into the brickwork. The tiles were put in at the request of Birmingham Corporation who believed that the roadway would be made lighter by their presence.

Holliday Street rises to meet Gas Street and Berkley Street. It is worth standing here for a moment and looking back at the aqueduct. The bottom part of Gas Street was originally the old Holliday Street and the entrance to the Gullet faced this part of Gas Street. When the Midland Railway made their new road, they built around the old Gullet, which presumably is still buried somewhere under the canal.

We cross Holliday Street to Holliday Street Wharf. The town of Birmingham had a public works depot here for many years. Stone was brought by canal barge to broken for use on the city streets.

The Holliday Street Depot was one of the first depots owned by the Public Works when it was set up in 1852. Initially it was only a small establishment which served the South and West Districts of the fledgling Borough of Birmingham, but grew in size and importance with the town.

Stables were provided from the start for the department's horses. There was a porter employed to weigh the corn, take account of the manure sold and measure out daily the corn for each horse. Another two men were used to clean the stables and feed the horses.

When Holliday Street was extended part of the wharf was taken to make the new street and this meant the demolition of buildings which then faced the old Holliday Street. The Midland Railway paid for what they took and it gave the Corporation opportunity to erect new buildings on the site. Amongst those constructed was a new stable block.

Holliday Street Wharf is now an Antique and Craft centre, where small traders sell there wares and antiques are sold in the former stables. In the centre on the yard are a row of stalls which are occupied by market traders on a Sunday. The craft stalls are located in the main building. There is also a cafe on the second floor. An entrance way leads on to canal towpath again.

The Worcester and Birmingham Canal passes behind Holliday Street Wharf and under Granville Street. The wharf opposite is now a boat repair yard and a number of craft regularly line the bank here. It is an old yard as the sign testifies. But it has not always been a boatyard. Doulton and Co used once the wharf as a pipe depot and before that it was a stone wharf.

Granville Street Bridge was rebuilt in the early 1870's. The original was narrow and hump-backed. The new bridge was built to accommodate a wider road, the canal and a railway line, hence the two arches.

Holliday Wharf was once a Corporation stone depot. There were also a large stable block for the horses which belonged to Birmingham Corporation.

DRAINAGE.

DOULTON's GLAZED STONEWARE PIPES and WATER CLOSET PANS may now be had at their Office and Depôt, GRANVILLE-STREET WHARF, BROAD-STREET, Birmingham.

The following Testimonial from J. PIGOTT SMITH, Esq., Town Surveyor of Birmingham, is respectfully submitted :—

"Commissioners of the Birmingham Street Act, Town Surveyor's Office, Moor-street, Birmingham, Oct. 22nd, 1849.

"Sir—I have much pleasure in bearing testimony to the very superior quality (both in material and workmanship) of the Glazed Sewage Pipes, made at your Rowley Regis Pottery. I have specified for their use in the Contracts let under the Commission, and recommend all parties to use them in the lateral drainage.

"I am, sir, your obedient servant,
"J. PIGOTT SMITH, Town Surveyor.
"Mr. H. Dalton, Sewage Pipe Pottery, Rowley Regis, Staffordshire."

An advertisement from the Birmingham Journal which refers to Doulton's pipe depot at Granville Street Wharf.

Granville Street crosses the canal by a wide brick bridge. It replaced the original narrow traditional hump-backed bridge when the West Suburban Railway was built. Granville Street Wharf, on the left of the picture, is now a boat yard.

The Birmingham West Suburban Railway was promoted by the Worcester and Birmingham Canal Company. It was intended to form a link from the London & North Western Railway station at New Street to the Midland Railway at Kings Norton. The ambitious scheme involved bridging Worcester Wharf.

After several modifications the railway was completed in 1876 from Kings Norton to Granville Street where a single platform station was built. The track was continued under Granville Street so that the engine could run round its train.

This piece of ground was once a burial ground for Jews. The remains had to be re-interred when the railway was constructed.

Granville Street station had only a short working life. Between 1882 and 1885 the Midland Railway constructed their own link into Birmingham by tunnelling under the canal. One line was made to Central Goods the other was driven from Five Ways through a series of tunnels into New Street. Granville Street Station was then closed but the track was retained as a storage siding. This siding was later known as Cemetery Siding after the former Jews cemetery.

From Granville Street to Gas St

Granville Street Bridge - Canal Towpath to Worcester Turn - Sharpness Company Toll Office - Bar Lock - Gas St.

We now follow the towpath back to Gas Street Basin and in a short distance reach the right angle bend in the canal which today is known as Worcester Turn. This place was also called Salvage Turn because the salvage boats once loaded there.

Opposite Worcester Turn were two canal basins also a right angles which increased the amount of canal frontage by a considerable amount. Many of the wharves in this area were taken as timber yards where fine foreign timber was often on sale. The Worcester and Birmingham Canal Co also had their main office here. It faced Blucher Street and had opened after the canal had been completed to Worcester.

A revision of the local rating system, led the Worcester and Birmingham Canal to re-site their headquarters. In 1864 new premises were constructed over their wharf in Gas Street and the Worcester Wharf offices were closed.

In 1874 the Gloucester & Berkeley Canal, Sharpness New Docks and Worcester and Birmingham Canal Navigation were incorporated by Act of Parliament into one concern. The new company adopted the rather lengthy title of the Sharpness New Docks & Gloucester & Birmingham Navigation Co which was regularly shortened to the Sharpness Company. A local committee of management was retained at the Gas Street Office to run the Worcester and Birmingham district.

At Worcester Turn there are a number of rails laid into the towpath. They were put there in June 1992 for perhaps cosmetic reasons. The rails once were located in the timber yard at Old Turn Junction.

The approach to the Bar Lock is in the shadow of warehouses now converted into a Nightclub. Part of these buildings were former stables erected by the Sharpness Company in 1876. They comprise the first building which joins the towpath after the aqueduct. Traces of the former stable doorways can still be seen even though they have now been bricked up.

On the opposite side of the canal are modern hotel and restaurants which are constructed to resemble old warehouses. In adopting these designs the architects have preserved a memory of the past. Pickford's and the Severn Carrying Company and several other carriers once had warehouses on this piece of the canal.

Salvage Turn in 1993. Modern buildings occupy what were timber wharves and a public wharf. The boats in the foreground are the modern equivalent of working boats. They were employed during 1993 to dredge the area around Gas Street and Worcester Bar.

The towpath from Salvage Turn to Gas Street has now been replaced with new bricks. it now a pleasant walk and many pause to talk the boaters.

The buildings on Worcester Wharf were demolished during the early 1970's. For a number of years, thereafter, boaters travelling along the Worcester and Birmingham were confronted with this sign at Salvage Turn advising them to slow down

The first carriers depots on Worcester Wharf had been established by 1800. Firms such as the Alvechurch Boat Company and the Hockley Boat Company were already in existence by that date and carrying on the canal.

By 1802 the Alvechurch Boat Company had started a packet boat from Birmingham to Hopwood which ran once a week. The Worcester and Birmingham Canal Company became concerned about the amount of damage the running of the packet did to the banks and increased their charges to the Alvechurch Company.

There are a mixture of buildings on the towpath side. Some are quite old. The building painted Arthurs Bar was a former Toll House built in 1876 for the Sharpness Company.

Next to the old toll office are the Worcester and Birmingham Canal Offices of 1864. It is worth pausing here for a moment. Note that windows are absent from a section of the wall, for here is actually a bricked up canal arm. These offices were built over the canal so as to reduce their local rate bill. The roving bridge which carried the towpath over the arm was removed when the basin was filled in.

On the other side of the Worcester & Birmingham Offices was another Toll Office built in 1893 for the Sharpness Company. This building replaced an earlier office which had fallen into disrepair. The new house comprised three floors. An entrance from the towpath led to the ground floor where the toll office was located. A second entrance was made from Gas Street to the first floor where the living accommodation was located. The second floor was reserved for the bedrooms. This Toll Office, which has now been converted into an Antique Shop, faces Worcester Bar.

The Bar Lock was the boundary between the two canals. Boats passing the lock in either direction were subject to the tolls of the canal they entered. When the lock was first made and a number of years afterwards there was an additional toll of 4d per ton on all coal and merchandise passing out of the Birmingham Canal. There was also a meter on the lock so that the Worcester Canal could be charged for the water they took from the Birmingham Canal.

A canal arm which came off the Worcester Canal served a square basin on the other side of Gas Street. It was completed during 1801 and provided wharf space for the Netherton Coal Company and the Birmingham Timber Company.

Much of the land from Broad Street to Holliday Street was leased in 1794 by the Timber Company from the Governors of King Edwards VI Grammar School. A separate lease was negotiated in 1800 for the Netherton Coal Company. The names on that lease were the same as the directors of the Dudley Canal Company.

It seems that the official title for this basin was the Netherton and it was the Netherton Coal Company which paid rates. However, as far as the Worcester and Birmingham Canal Company were concerned, it was the Dudley Canal who were responsible for maintenance of the new basin.

In 1816 the Birmingham Timber Company decided to cease trading and advertised their wharves and other property for sale. At this time Gas Street was just a crude way leading from Broad Street to the Worcester & Birmingham Company wharves at Holliday Street. It did not even have a name, although there were plans to call it Netherton Street.

The British Waterways Bridge Street Depot occupied a long length of canal frontage. They were the last owners of the depot which had been enlarged and extended by the Severn Carrying Company. At an earlier time there were a number of independent carriers depots located here which included Pickford's and William Partridge.

Courtesy Birmingham Library.

A 1978 view of the cobbled towpath near the Bar Lock.

In Support of a Bill for establishing a Navigable Communication between the Birmingham Canal Navigations and the Worcester and Birmingham Canal.

The Marquis of Buckingham, The Earl of Coventry, Sir Charles Mordaunt, Bart. Mr. Dugddale Stratford Dugdale, Mr. Charles Mills, Mr. Frankland Lewis, Mr. W. Duff Gordon, Mr. Manning, Mr. Howarth Mr. Roberts, The Hon. Henry Legge, The Hon. Admiral Sir A. Kaye Legge, The Honorable and very Rev. the Dean of Windsor, The Honorable and Rev. Archdeacon Legge, the Birmingham Canal Company, and the Worcester and Birmingham Canal Company, request the favor of your attendance on the Second Reading of the Bill, which is fixed for Tuesday the 7th March, 1815, at 4 o'Clock.

The proposal to breach the Worcester Bar and create a lock attracted a lot of powerful support as this card shows. *Courtesy Birmingham Library Archives.*

The towpath from Salvage Turn to the Bar Lock has been improved within the last few years. This 1984 view illustrates the extent of that change.

The facade of the later Worcester and Birmingham Canal Company office in Gas Street. The canal arm which first served the Netherton Coal Company wharves and later the Gasworks passed under the road at this place. Only the raised footpath remains to indicate its course.

In 1817, a Gasworks was established at the bottom of the street by John Gostling. It was private venture, which became a public concern in 1819 when the Birmingham Gas Light and Coke Company purchased the works. The crude way became known as Gas Street, a name which it has carried to the present day.

Walking through the passageway between the old canal offices and the first toll office, Gas Street is reached. Opposite are buildings which formerly belonged to W.H.Fraley, now disused. The arm of the canal which passed under the Canal Offices continued under Gas Street and through Fraley's Yard.

One of the former Fraley buildings has a round roof very much in the style of other canal-side structures which once lined Gas Street basin. Next to is another and evidently older building. Though much altered, this structure was first erected as a retort house for the Gas Works. The iron roof supports can still be seen inside.

In the 1990's many people associate gas with the natural gas taken from the North Sea, but in the early nineteenth century gas was made from coal by a process developed by William Murdoch. The first gas produced was used for lighting and the by-product coke was sold for industrial use. Only later was gas adapted for cooking and heating purposes.

Coal had to be brought to the gasworks in order that gas might be made. The Birmingham works utilised a local coal merchant, John Wynne, for the initial supplies, but as demand increased greater amounts of coal were required. Coal began to arrive at the Netherton Basin. It was then taken along a short railway to the retort house, which lay at the bottom of Gas Street. In 1822, a new and larger retort house was built closer to the Netherton Basin. It is this second retort house, which survives today. More land was acquired and eventually the gasworks occupied all the land between Gas Street and Berkley St west of the canal basin.

A second canal basin crossed Gas Street and joined with the Birmingham Canal on their side of the Bar Lock. This was a private cut made about 1795 to provide a wharf for the Timber Company.

Another wharf, on the opposite side of the basin, was used by John Wynne, the coal merchant. John Wynne died in 1817, and his wharf appears then to have been taken over by John Danks, merchandise carrier.

John Greaves acquired the property located between the two basins in 1824. He was interested in bringing bricks, lime and coal to Birmingham and set up a carriers business here. It is probable that he was helped in this task by Robert Rymill Judd. Greaves had lent Robert money after his father, William Judd was made bankrupt.

About 1825 both basins were extended in length under Berkley Street. They provided accommodation for coal merchants, lime merchants and carriers. Greaves allowed another carrier, Moses Robinson, wharf space in the former Netherton Basin.

Traders continued to use the basins until about 1840, while coal, lime and bricks were brought in till at least 1850. Isaac Flavell had a brick wharf on the Netherton Arm about this time. He carried bricks from his brick works above Lappal Tunnel.

During the 1850's the nature of traffic to these wharves changed as new firms were established beside them. At the end of the former Netherton Basin, on the far side of Berkley Street, Walter May established the Suffolk Works where he manufactured steam engines and boilers. Many of the raw components evidently came in by boat.

A few yards down Berkley Street was Thomas Worsdell's works which constructed railway waggons, cranes and the odd steam locomotive. Richard Cadbury Gibbins later took over Worsdell's and May's works and developed an important crane building works on their sites and other surrounding property. Some of the cranes manufactured by Gibbins went to canal side warehouses; there is one at Tardebigge, for example.

The Gas Works ceased production in 1850 and although the holders were retained for a number of years, parts of the other buildings found other uses. The retort house and wharf land between the canal basins were taken for a tube works.

Sampson Hanbury, George Selby and Thomas Barclay erected rolling mills and engines on the site and set up the Imperial Tube Company on this site. About 1877, Selby left the partnership and his place was taken by Thomas Turley. The name of the firm then changed to the Anchor Tube Company.

The tube works operated until 1911, when the site was taken over by Fraley. There are still remnants of a 16in gauge railway on the site which was probably adapted from the earlier gasworks railway. The railway seems to have been used by the Anchor Tube Company to carry material from the canal basin to different parts of the works.

Fraley's offices, which stand on the land between the basins, were previously used as offices by the Anchor Tube Works. They were once longer than they now are. The original building formerly extended across the basin which lies nearest Broad Street.

On the Broad Street side of second basin was a lead works occupied by Stock and Taylor. Lead was brought by boats from Bristol to these works.

We continue along Gas St towards Broad Street. An entrance on the wall leads back onto the canal. Before we enter it is worth pausing to look at the group of old buildings which front the canal. Those which face Broad St are the most modern, the rest are much older. The white building was formerly a seed merchants and another was known as the Navigation Inn. Note the BCN boundary post set in the wall.

In front of these buildings were once three cab stands. In the days before motorised transport, there were a number of these stands placed around the city. Here the horse-drawn Hackney Carriages would wait for a fare.

W.H.Fraley's stone yard before closure. Marble was cut and shaped in an open yard which lay between the two canal basins.

A recent view of Worcester Bar which shows the BCN and Worcester & Birmingham Toll Offices on the right of the picture.

Another view of the two toll offices from the canal-side.

From Gas Street to Centenary Square

Gas Street - Worcester Bar - Bridge Street - Broad Street - Centenary Square.

The gate in the wall leads on to the top of the roving bridge which spanned the old Timber Company basin. A rough cobbled way worn by the passage of many boat horses lead down to the towpath. We turn right and climb the bridge over the Bar Lock. Before this bridge was provided the task of crossing the canal involved a precarious walk along a footbridge.

At the far end of the bridge is a parapet which provides a good vantage point to survey the whole of Gas Street Basin. The old canal side buildings which face Gas Street appear much taller from the towpath side. Some of these buildings pre-date 1850 and may be much older.

When the Birmingham Canal was first built in 1773, it curved round to reach the Old Wharf. On the outside of the curve were built two boat docks, which are believed to have been used by Canal Company for their own boats. In those days Gas Street was merely a rough road to serve these docks.

One of the docks was removed when the cut was made into the Timber Company land, the other remained and was let in 1797 to Robert Skey. He, in turn, appears to have sub let it to George Ryder Bird for a boat building business. No towpath then existed on this side of the canal and the land beside Gas Street was then occupied by wharves and warehouses.

One wharf belonged to the carrier Henry Weeks. He advertised that his wharf lay opposite the Brasshouse. It would appear that it was on the piece of land between Gas Street and the canal.

The construction of the Bar Lock in 1815 changed the local wharf geography quite considerably. The lock was made across Worcester Bar and the remaining dock removed. A BCN Toll Office was built so that the Birmingham Canal could gauge all boats passing through. That toll office, now painted white, still stands at the head of the Bar Lock.

We now proceed down the walk-way from the bridge down onto Worcester Bar. Boats still moor on the Bar and pontoons have now been installed so that people can walk clear of the boats tied up there.

When the canal was first proposed from Birmingham to Worcester the BCN refused to allow any scheme which might join their canal and deprive it of water. The Worcester & Birmingham Canal obtained their Act of Parliament in 1791 and construction began at the Birmingham

No.6, ACHILLES, moored alongside the cottages at Gas Street. She is a butty which belongs to the Birmingham & Midland Carrying and is still used to ferry spoil and rubbish when needed.

Second City Canal Cruises are one of the two surviving trip boat operators. Their office were located in the basement of a canal cottage in Gas Street. They have now moved to Kingston Row.

end. It was not until the 30th October 1795 that the first part of the canal was opened between Birmingham and Selly Oak and Kings Norton was reached the following year.

A physical bar 7ft 3in wide and 84 yards long was constructed so that no craft could pass between the BCN and the Worcester and Birmingham. All goods travelling over the two canals had to be transhipped from one boat to another.

The Worcester & Birmingham Canal took many years to complete. Inflation had caused the cost of construction to rise many times, but eventually, in 1815 the job was done. A shorter route was offered to the River Severn than hitherto had existed and several important Iron and Coal Masters brought pressure to bear on the BCN to remove the Bar so that through traffic could be established. The Worcester & Birmingham Company, themselves, also made repeated requests to BCN and eventually sought an Act of Parliament to breach it. This received royal assent in 1815 and the bar lock was constructed.

We continue along the Bar past all the moored boats. The path leads through another gate beside the James Brindley and from here to Bridge Street where we turn left.

On the right was the site of the Old Wharf and now is the Central Television Studios. The Old Wharf occupied a piece of land near the corner of Broad Street and Suffolk Street. It was enclosed on the Broad Street side by the Eagle Foundry. About 1856 property in Broad Street and Suffolk Street was taken for a row of elegant looking buildings which became known as Broad Street Corner.

Coal was the chief commodity handled here. Upwards of sixty coal merchants used the Old Wharf at any one time. The traffic in coal to these wharves was tremendous. But, railway competition gradually took this traffic off the canal and the number of merchants using the wharf dwindled.

Large stocks of coal were always on hand at the wharf. Merchants sold the coal the their customers which was then carted to them. There was a clerk employed by the BCN to accurately weigh the coal going out of the wharf. He handed the carter a ticket which was passed on to the customer. Those who bought the coal were thus assured that they received the correct weight of coal.

Of course, no system is fool proof as Joseph Fisher proved in 1825. Fisher was a coal merchant who managed to steal a blank book of tickets from the weighing machine house.

Joseph Fisher employed Richard Kinching as his carter and it was Kinching's job to deliver the coals to the customers. But, Richard, rarely handed over the weighing machine ticket, usually it was brought by Fisher later.

Worcester Bar in 1979. A number of boats moored alongside were used as floating homes.

Worcester Bar in 1993 presents a very different scene to that in 1979. A number of vessels are seen at the Bar, but they are now moored to pontoons .

Fisher, in reality, brought with him a new ticket with the weights altered upwards in his favour. He was therefore paid more for the coals and pocketed the difference. The fraud went on for a year before it was discovered.

William Robinson, a coachmaker from Slaney Street, noticed the coal he had bought was being used too quickly. He checked and reported the matter to the BCN. Fisher was arrested and sent for trial at Warwick Assizes. Joseph was found guilty and sentenced to 7 years transportation.

In 1912 the BCN closed their offices on the Old Wharf and moved them to Daimler House in Paradise Street. Boats continued to bring coal into the wharf until about 1926 when the whole site was sold to Birmingham Corporation for the new Civic Centre. The wharf was then filled and the old offices demolished. For a number of years later, what had been the Old Wharf served Birmingham as a car park until the present buildings were erected.

In 1847 John Cadbury moved his tea and cocoa business from Bull Street to Bridge Street. The factory was located at 4 Bridge Street and backed onto the towpath of the Old Wharf.

John lost interest in the firm after his wife died, and handed the control of the business to two of his sons George and Richard. The Cadbury brothers after initial problems eventually made the venture a success. In 1879 they transferred to Bournville. Later, part of the Bridge Street premises were let to William Pearce.

The walk continues past the Hyatt Regency Hotel to Broad Street. The buildings on this side of the street have a relatively modern history. Originally a number of premises stood here numbered from 297 to 316. At the end were the separate Broad Street Corner Buildings. At 310 was the White Hart Inn.

Behind the White Hart was Smith and Hawkes Eagle Foundry. This works produced a range of metal goods which were often shipped to their destination by canal boat. The Foundry was demolished during the 1920's to make way for other buildings.

The modern Broad Street frontage has buildings which were designed in the fashion of original Civic Centre Scheme. They include the Municipal Bank, built in 1932, a Masonic Hall which is now the Central Television Offices and the Registry Office.

We now cross Broad Street to return to Centenary Square and the starting point of the walk.

A bill head from John Stokes who was a coal and coke dealer at the Old Wharf which the Birmingham Canal Navigations offices.

This view of Bridge Street looking towards Broad Street dates from about 1910. The building on the right behind the waggon formerly belonged to Cadbury Brothers.

Courtesy Cadbury Ltd

CANAL CARRYING AND CANAL TRADERS

There are two sorts of canals which exist in Britain today, narrow and wide. At strategic points the narrow canals join either wide canals or rivers. For boaters who use the waterway, these junctions are well known.

To the carriers and traders who once used the canal such places provided obstacles to their trade. Goods often had to be transhipped into larger vessel and other people involved. The domain of the narrow boat was generally confined to the centre of England where a complex system of canals developed to serve mainly the needs of industry.

Birmingham lies at the crossroads of the narrow canals network and is the meeting point of a number of canals. These waterway form link in a chain which connects London with Manchester and Liverpool.

Todays canals are the result of many men hopes and dreams to improve the transport system which then prevailed. The first canals came into being to provide an alternative to the muddy and clogged roads of the period. Many of these original canals were designed by James Brindley and although practical for time often followed a circuitous path. The second generation of canals came about during the 1790's. They gave shorter and more direct routes to the towns and cities they served.

The trading and canal carrying business grew as the canals developed and this is reflected in the numbers of traders who establish depots in Birmingham. In 1800 there was a only a trickle, but by 1820 there was a flood. It was cut-throat competition at a time when the economy had suffered through a prolonged war with the French. Several carriers faced bankruptcy but there were others who were willing to take their place.

Some of the earliest carriers started on the roads and extended their trade to the canals when they were built. Where this happened they usually maintained their fleet of road waggons and used them to meet their boats at strategic places to serve towns and villages away from the line of the canal. When the canals were ice bound or shut through stoppages, these carriers could still provide a service by road to their customers.

It was common to find that carriers formed partnerships amongst themselves. Sometimes associations were formed between carriers based in different parts of the country who usually traded on different routes. Their combined efforts meant they could advertise a better service. There was the added advantage that each had access to the others wharves and thereby avoided otherwise expensive wharf charges. Other partnerships were formed by people with the same interest in mind. Often they were new to the trade and used their assets to set up in business together.

A third generation of canal building began during the 1820's in a vain attempt to stave off competition from the railways. These, again provided shorter routes or improved existing canals.

The railways took a lot of trade from the canals, but certain bulk items such as chemicals, coal, iron goods and salt continued to be carried by water.

Some traders took on the dual role of a railway and canal carrier for a while. Gradually they disappeared and by 1880 only a handful of dedicated canal carriers remained. Through mergers and amalgamations large canal carrying concerns had grown out of ashes of the small.

Birmingham had its share of commercial, or merchandise, carriers whose depots were the waterside wharves and basins near the city centre. A list of the carriers who used the wharves in the Gas Street area now follows to illustrate the variety of people who were involved with the carrying trade. It should be noted that this not a complete list of the Birmingham carriers and only relates to the trail previously discussed. There were other important depots at Aston Junction, Fazeley Street and Salford Bridge. There were also many other carriers who navigated the waters around Gas Street.

In addition to the commercial carriers, there were numerous coal merchants, iron manufacturers and several lime merchants who used their own craft. Bricks, salt and sand were commodities often carried in private vessels.

As late as 1920 canal carrying was still and important business, then the decline set in. The sharpest drop in trade was between 1930 and 1950. What little trade that was left was finally lost in the bitter winter of 1963. Some carrying still goes on, but the canals are now the domain of the pleasure boat.

The Birmingham & Midland Canal Carrying Company started as commercial carriers but now operate a number of trip and camping boats which are often seen at Gas Street.

LIST OF CARRIERS

A list of merchandise carriers is given below. The location of their depots, where known, are denoted by the following abbreviations.

BK   Berkley and Gas St Wharves
BS   Broad Street
C   Crescent Wharves (originally Farmers Wharf)
FB   Friday Bridge
GS   Great Charles Street
OW   Old Wharf, Paradise Street
SW   Sherborne Wharf, Sherborne Street
WW   Worcester Wharf, Bridge Street

ADAM, SOUTHERN & CO   GS

Operated from Great Charles for only a couple of years. They ceased trading in 1803. Their boats were auctioned on 8th December.

THOMAS ADAMS   C   FB

Adams operated between Birmingham and Walsall. He used Judd's at the Crescent c1808 - 1814, then Mrs Swaine's wharf at Friday Bridge.

ANTWIS & STURLAND   C

Antwis & Sturland took over Benjamin Bradley's trade to Manchester during 1820. They occupied two adjacent wharves at the Crescent, one on the Newhall branch, the other on the basin which led to Gibson's Arm. This firm was later carried on as Tildasley and Sturland.

ASHWIN & CO   WW

Ashwin & Co established a depot at Worcester Wharf c1850. Goods were consigned along the Worcester & Birmingham and Stratford - upon - Avon canals and also onto the River Avon. About 1860 they became the Stratford -upon- Avon Canal Carrying Co.

BARKER, CARTER & ALLEN   BS

Barker, Carter & Co were Sandbach canal traders who used a wharf in Broad Street 1830-1831. Their wharf was taken over by Shipton & Co in September 1831.

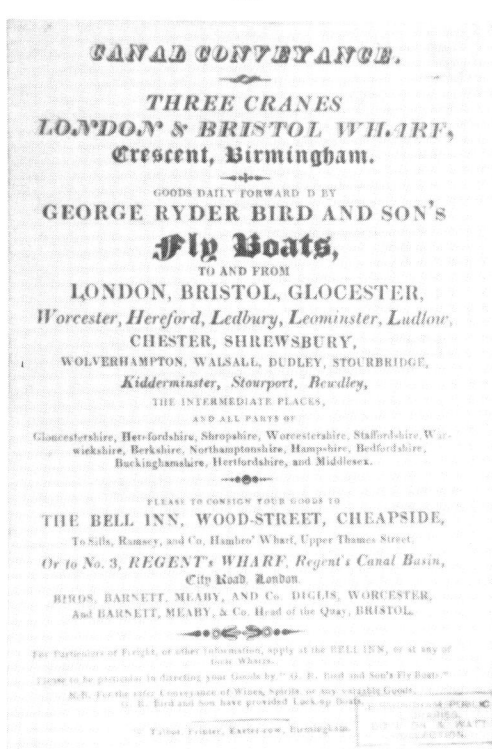

CANAL CONVEYANCE.

THREE CRANES
LONDON & BRISTOL WHARF,
Crescent, Birmingham.

GOODS DAILY FORWARDED BY
GEORGE RYDER BIRD AND SON's
Fly Boats,
TO AND FROM
LONDON, BRISTOL, GLOCESTER,
Worcester, Hereford, Ledbury, Leominster, Ludlow,
CHESTER, SHREWSBURY,
WOLVERHAMPTON, WALSALL, DUDLEY, STOURBRIDGE,
Kidderminster, Stourport, Bewdley,
THE INTERMEDIATE PLACES,
AND ALL PARTS OF
Gloucestershire, Herefordshire, Shropshire, Worcestershire, Staffordshire, Warwickshire, Berkshire, Northamptonshire, Hampshire, Bedfordshire, Buckinghamshire, Hertfordshire, and Middlesex.

PLEASE TO CONSIGN YOUR GOODS TO
THE BELL INN, WOOD-STREET, CHEAPSIDE,
To Sills, Ramsey, and Co, Hambro' Wharf, Upper Thames Street,
Or to No. 3, REGENT's WHARF, Regent's Canal Basin,
City Road, London.
BIRDS, BARNETT, MEABY, AND Co. DIGLIS, WORCESTER,
And BARNETT, MEABY, & Co. Head of the Quay, BRISTOL.

For Particulars of Freight, or other Information, apply at the BELL INN, or at any of their Wharfs.
Please to be particular in directing your Goods by "G. R. Bird and Son's Fly Boats."
N.B. For the safer Conveyance of Wines, Spirits, or any valuable Goods, G. R. Bird and Son have provided Lock-up Boats.

Talbot, Printer, Exeter-row, Birmingham.

A card advertising the service offered by George Ryder Bird, now in the Boulton & Watt collection. *Courtesy Birmingham Library Archives.*

15/26

G. R. BIRD and SON respectfully give Notice, that all Goods received by them for the Purpose of being carried, will be considered as General Liens, and will, at their Option, be held until Payment, not only of the Money due for the Carriage of such particular Goods, but also for all Sums of Money then or thereafter to become due to them from the Owners of the said Goods; and if not redeemed in one Month, will be sold to defray such General Balance. No Claim for Loss or Damage will be allowed, unless made in Writing within three Days after the Goods are delivered. All Goods carried on the Severn or other rivers will be at the Risque of the respective Owners thereof, agreeable to the Public Notice of the Severn Carriers in general. G. R. BIRD and SON will not be accountable for any Loss or Damage happening by Fire, nor for any Package containing Money in Cash or Bills, Jewellery, Bullion, Plate, Watches, Rings, Lace, Furs, Writings, Prints, Paintings, China, Glass, Wearing Apparel, Musical Instruments, Furniture, Toys, or any other valuable Articles, in Packages or otherwise, unless the same be insured according to their Value, and paid for at the Time of Delivery. Goods packed in returned Packages or Wrappers, if lost or damaged, will not be paid for.

M

To G. R. BIRD AND SON, for Freight, &c. Dr.

Date.		From.	T.	C.	Q.	lb.	Rate.	Paid on.	£	s.	d.

A bill from by George Ryder Bird & Sons for packages carried in 1833 from London to the Botanical Gardens in Birmingham. *Courtesy Birmingham Library Archives.*

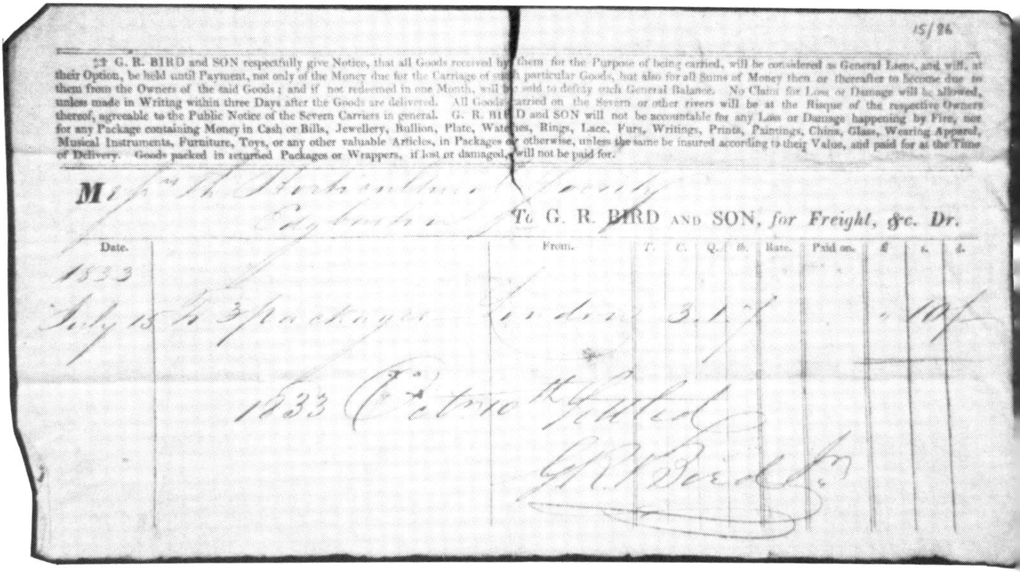

GEORGE RYDER BIRD & SONS   BS   C

George Ryder Bird was a Shropshire man, Bridgnorth born and bred. His unusual middle name was actually his mothers maiden name and it was George's choice to pass this middle name on to his children and sometimes even the grand-children. George started as a boat builder and by 1800 had established a boat building business at Broad Street. About 1804 Bird joined Robert Skey in partnership became a carrier. This partnership was to last till June 1811 when he set up on his own account at Broad Street Wharf. In 1814 Bird took over Judd's wharf at the Crescent. Bird traded extensively on the canals and carried goods to Liverpool, London, Manchester, Worcester and Stourport. His wharf at the Crescent was sometimes known as the London and Bristol Wharf because this formed the basis of his trade. A more popular title was the Three Cranes Wharf which is taken from a wharf in London which he used. George Ryder Bird's family helped him manage his business, particularly his eldest son, George Ryder. George, senior, died in 1837 only to be followed in 1838 by George Ryder Bird Junior. After his death, the trade was taken over by James Shipton.

BIRMINGHAM CARRYING COMPANY   C

A firm, known by this title, commenced as general carriers at the start of October 1806 and advertised a service to London and Oxford. They may have been connected with William Judd & Son.

BRADLEY AND CO   BS   C   GC

Benjamin Bradley was a canal agent turned carrier who specialised in the Liverpool and Manchester trade. During his working career, Bradley used a number of wharves in the Birmingham area. Benjamin often traded of partnership with others. He first had the use of a wharf at the top of Great Charles Street and was handling merchandise there by 1805. Bradley was later joined in partnership by Thomas Coleman. About 1814 Benjamin Bradley joined Thomas Crockett and Francis Sakeld at Aston Junction and left Coleman at Great Charles Street. From October 1816 Bradley was on his own again and his boats loaded the at the wharf in Broad Street and later at the Crescent. During 1820 Antwiss & Sturland took over Benjamin Bradley's carrying trade and the wharf he then used at the Crescent.

BRIDGEWATER NAVIGATION CO LTD   GC

The Duke of Bridgewater's Trustees owned and operated the Bridgewater Canal which connected Manchester with Liverpool. They took over Worthington's carrying business in 1849 and continued to use the Great Charles Street Wharf. In 1872 the Birmingham and Wolverhampton canal carrying trade passed to the Bridgewater Navigation Co who disposed of it during 1879 to Fellows, Morton & Co.

JAMES BROMLEY   C   WW

James Bromley was a Worcester carrier who traded along the Worcester & Birmingham Canal. He took over Skey's warehouse on Worcester Wharf during 1819. Bromley also had the use of Wheatcroft's wharf at the Crescent. He offered a daily fly boat service to Worcester and by 1825 was in partnership with a gentleman named Hood.

HUMPHREY BROWN & Co   BK

Brown operated narrow boat service to Worcester, barges on the River Severn and coastal trading ships. He used Berkley Street Canal Wharf c1828-1834.

JOHN CHAMBERS   WW

John Chambers was a wharfinger at Worcester Wharf c1820-c1825 who carried goods to Stratford-upon-Avon and then along the Avon to Evesham.

CHESTER & LIVERPOOL LIGHTERAGE & WAREHOUSE CO LTD   C

This firm, registered in 1921, came to deal with the Shropshire Union Railway & Canal Company traffic when the Shropshire Company ceased trading. They operated from two of the former Shropshire Union wharves at the Crescent 1922- 1931.

COLEMAN & INGLEBY   GS

Thomas Coleman & Thomas Ingleby set up as carriers c1814 at wharf formerly used by Benjamin Bradley. Coleman was made bankrupt in June 1817. The fleet of 9 boats and stock in was sold off to pay the creditors.

CROCKETT & SALKELD   GS

Thomas Crockett and Francis Salkeld were Liverpool and Manchester carriers who operated their own flats between Runcorn and the Port of Liverpool. They moved to Great Charles Street in 1817 after Coleman & Ingleby gave up the trade. T Crockett used this wharf until 1830. The warehouse, counting house, waggons and seven waggon horses were sold by auction 11/06/1830.

EXPEDITIOUS CANAL CONVEYANCE
TO AND FROM
London ; for Salop, Wolverhampton and Birmingham

THE WOLVERHAMPTON BOAT COMPANY

trust from the very liberal Encouragement they have experienced, that the Goods consigned to their boats have been conveyed to the Satisfaction of their friends; they further assure them that no Exertion shall be wanting on their Part to ensure Regularity and Expedition, and thereby merit a Continuance of their favours.

Their FLY BOATS will continue to sail from Bickley and Co's Wharf, Wolverhampton for London (with or without loading) every Tuesday and Friday Mornings, by which Goods will be conveyed without being unloaded until they arrive at their Wharf, Paddington; from whence they will meet a speedy and punctual delivery.

Boats load at the Company's Wharf, Paddington, every Tuesday and Friday , for Birmingham, Wolverhampton and Salop. By these boats Goods are regularly conveyed to London from the undermentioned Places and from London for the same:-

Atherstone	Coventry	Stourport
Blisworth	Dudley	Stafford
Braunstone	Gloucester	Shrewsbury
Brentford	Leicester	Wolverhampton
Birmingham	Lichfield	Walsall
Bridgnorth	Kidderminster	Worcester
Bromsgrove	Stourbridge	Uxbridge, &c.

Their Stage Boats will load as under; from Wolverhampton to Birmingham, every Tuesday and Friday; from Birmingham to Wolverhampton, every Monday and Thursday; from Birmingham to Stourbridge every Tuesday and Friday; also a Boat from Birmingham to Walsall every Tueday and Friday.

Mr Young's Waggon loads at Bickley and Co's Wharf, Wolverhampton, every Tuesday and Friday, by which goods are conveyed to Shiffnal, Wellington, Salop and all Parts of North Wales, with the utmost Expidition.

Goods Taken in, and daily Attendance given , at the following Places:-

Salop, G.Young's Warehouse
Wolverhampton, Bickley and Co's Wharf
Tipton Green, W.Pitchfork's Wharf
Stourport, S Danks and Co's Wharf
Walsall, T.Adams's Wharf
Stourbridge, J.Weston's Wharf
Birmingham, the Company's Warehouse, Crescent Wharf
Paddington, Company Wharf, Bridge Wharf, Harrow Road
London, Salisbury Arms, Cow Lane, West Smithfield

Lock up boats are provided for the safe conveyance of Wines and Spirits

When the Canals are rendered impassable by Frost, or otherwise, the Company will (if required) forward Goods by Land at Land Rate.

For Further Particulars apply to John Crowley, Wolverhampton, Wolverhampton; or to the Company's Agent, Mr John Scott, Salisbury Arms, London.

Wolverhampton March 2 1807.

An advertisement published in Aris's Gazette, March 9 1807 which concerns the service offered by the Wolverhampton Boat Company, later Crowley & Hicklin.

CROWLEY, HICKLIN & CO   C

Crowley, Hicklin & Co were Wolverhampton carriers. They started as the Wolverhampton Boat Co and by 1805 had commenced a fly boat service from Wolverhampton to London. Their first Birmingham depot was at W Dones wharf, Aston Junction. In 1806, they moved to the Crescent where a wharf was leased from Charles Norton and a warehouse constructed. It was situated between Norton's lime wharves and Sherratt's depot. John Crowley was the Wolverhampton agent for the Boat Company. He and Benjamin Hicklin carried on the trade from 1811 under their own names. They were later joined by William Batty. New trading routes were established which included Liverpool and Manchester. By 1830, the firm traded extensively. John Crowley died in 1843, but the business was continued in his name. Crowley and Co later became railway carriers, but retained their wharf at the Crescent until c1872.

JOHN DANKS   BK   GC

The two business's of Samuel Danks & Co at Gas Street and Heath, Tyler and Danks at Great Charles Street became known as John Danks from 1831. Generally the Gas Street Wharf handled the traffic for Bristol and Worcester, whilst the Great Charles Street Depot dealt with the Manchester and Nottingham trades. John Danks is best considered as a Birmingham carrier, because it was in Birmingham and later Harborne where he lived with his family. John gave up the business about 1844 and the two Birmingham depots were closed. Other branches of the Danks family continued in the canal trade from Stourport as Danks, Venn, and Sanders.

SAMUEL DANKS & CO   BK   BS

There is a complicated history behind the inception of the firm of Samuel Danks & Company. Samuel Danks was a Wednesbury Coal master who owned mines at Monway Field. He entered the canal carrying business in partnership with John Wall who traded as Wall & Co from the Broad Street Wharf. By 1798 Samuel operated under his own name, but continued to share the wharf in Broad Street with Wall. Successive generations of the Danks family were involved with the trade at Birmingham and Stourport. They owned barges for the River Severn and narrow boats for the canal traffic. Samuel died in 1805, but the trade was continued by John Danks, Isaiah Danks and a Stourport carrier Edmund Tyler under the name Samuel Danks & Co. John Danks was manager of the Broad Street depot. Danks & Co later transferred across to the Islington Basin in Gas Street. Their wharf on Broad Street, which was sub let to a Mr Kendrick, corn dealer, was offered for sale in May 1830. Isaiah Danks also traded under the title of Bickley, Danks & Co from Wolverhampton. Isaiah Danks left

Wolverhampton during 1831 and set up another canal business at Stourport with Thomas Yandell Venn. They operated as Isaiah Danks, Venn & Co.

DEAN & CO   C

John Dean used Wheatcroft's wharf at the Crescent c1815-1816. Goods were conveyed to Warwick, Banbury and Oxford.

JAMES & JOHN DEYKIN   C

John Deykin established a carrying business to Oxford and London about 1807. He used a wharf next to Judd's. James Deykin was a road carrier who took over from John Deykin c1811. A partner in this concern was William Deykin.

THOMAS DIXON & CO   BK

T. Dixon took over Henry Week's business in 1807 and traded from the Islington Wharf to Worcester until c1812. Dixon worked in conjunction with Cresswell and Barnes who operated trows on the Severn from Worcester to Bristol.

GIBBINS, SMALL & CO   BS

This firm was created about 1813 when James Gibbins, Thomas Small, George Blount and Moses Robinson went into partnership together. They became carriers, wharfingers and dealers in coal and iron at Birmingham, Stourport and Wolverhampton. Gibbins, Small & Co took over the wharf and warehouse used by Robert Skey and traded to London and Stourport. The partnership was dissolved on 21st December 1815, when George Blount left, but the remaining partners continued to carry as Gibbins & Co during 1816. By 1817 the business was in the hands of Moses Robinson.

J FELLOWS & CO   WW

Joshua Fellows was a Tipton carrier who managed the business established by his father, James, in 1837. Joshua and his younger brother James were to develop an important canal business which included the trade to Worcester, Gloucester and Stourport. By 1863 J Fellows & Co had rented part of the No.4 Worcester Wharf and had commenced to trade along the Worcester & Birmingham Canal. This trade was increased in March 1868 when they acquired the business of the Worcester Carrying Co. In 1873, Joshua and James Fellows went into partnerships with Danks and Sanders to form the Severn & Canal Carrying, Shipping and Steam Towing Co Ltd. The Worcester trade then passed into the hands of the new concern. Joshua Fellows also continued to trade under the title of the Trustees of James Fellows & Co until 1876.

Fellows Morton & Clayton owned a large fleet of vessels including some steam powered craft. PRESIDENT has been restored to working order and is sometimes seen on the local canal system. She is shown here approaching St Vincent Street Bridge.

FELLOWS, MORTON & CO   GC

Joshua Fellows went into partnership with Fred Morton in 1876. Fellows, Morton & Co became agents for the Bridgewater Navigation Co and handled all their traffic from Great Charles Street. Three depots were now maintained by this firm; Bridgewater Wharf, Great Charles Street; Toll End, Tipton and Wolverhampton.

FELLOWS MORTON & CLAYTON   C   SW

Fellows, Morton & Co merged with William Clayton, the Saltley based carrier in 1889 to form Fellows, Morton & Clayton Ltd. William Clayton had died in 1882 ,but his business had been carried on by a son, Thomas Clayton who became a director of the new concern together with Joshua Fellows and Frederick Morton. The Great Charles Street wharf was given up and the Birmingham business concentrated at Park Wharf, Saltley. Fellows, Morton and Clayton became the biggest canal carrying concern in this country. Apart from their midland based activities they had depots in Leicester, Liverpool, London, Manchester, Northampton and Nottingham. About 1924 they took over two wharves at the Crescent, Birmingham from the Shropshire Union Company. In 1938 they built a new warehouse and wharf at Sherborne Street. They ceased trading in 1949 when their depots, fleet of boats and other property was taken over by the Docks & Inland Waterways Executive.

GRAND JUNCTION CANAL CO   C

The Grand Junction Canal Company took over the business of John Whitehouse & Sons in 1848 and used their wharf at the Crescent until 1849. They then transferred their Birmingham depot to Fazeley Street.

JOHN GREAVES   BK

John Greaves was a Commission Agent, Factor, Corn Merchant and Wharfinger at Berkley St. He purchased the former Dudley Canal Company/Timber Wharf in Gas Street during 1824 and used it for the coal and brick trade.

R.GREAVES   BK

Richard Greaves used John Greaves wharf to provide a carrying service to Stratford-upon-Avon and Moreton-in-Marsh during the 1830's.

JOHN HALLAN   GC

A Hull carrier whose boats loaded at Dank's Wharf c1833-1835.

J.HARDY   WW

A carrier who operated to Stratford -upon- Avon c1830.

HEATH, TYLER & DANKS   GC

Operated from Great Charles St Wharf and took over the Birmingham trade from Hugh Henshall & Co although Henshall remained their landlord at Great Charles Street. Matthew Heath left the partnership and concentrated on his Stourport business. They then traded as Danks, Tyler & Danks for a time. From 1831 this business was simply carried on under the name of John Danks.

HUGH HENSHALL   GC

Hugh Henshall traded on the Birmingham Canal as soon as it was completed. In 1777 a wharf at the top of Great Charles Street was leased from the Colmore family. Henshall carried goods over the full length of the Trent and Mersey Navigation, Staffordshire & Worcester Canal and the Birmingham Canal and used upwards of eighty boats to maintain the service. The Birmingham trade was let to Heath, Tyler & Danks in 1812.

RICHARD JUDD   FB

The road and canal carrying business established by William Judd was continued under the name of Richard Judd from 1814 until 1819. Richard, a son of William, had looked after the family affairs in Birmingham and both he and his father were made bankrupt in 1814. The new business was incorporated under the names of Richard's half brother Robert Rymill Judd and Henry Stone. Robert Rymill Judd was then a grazier, whilst Henry Stone was a grocer. Robert borrowed money on the strength of a legacy, due to him, to assist him with the business. This debt was taken over by John Greaves in 1819 who apparently used it as means to acquire their boats for his own purposes. Henry Stone later purchased the road haulage part of the business, while the Oxford canal trade and wharves were taken by Crowley, Hicklin & Co. Robert Rymill Judd stayed in Birmingham and set up a corn merchants business in Jamaica Row.

WILLIAM JUDD & SONS   C

William was a Banbury road haulier who operated a service from Thomas Taylor's warehouse at the top of New Street, in

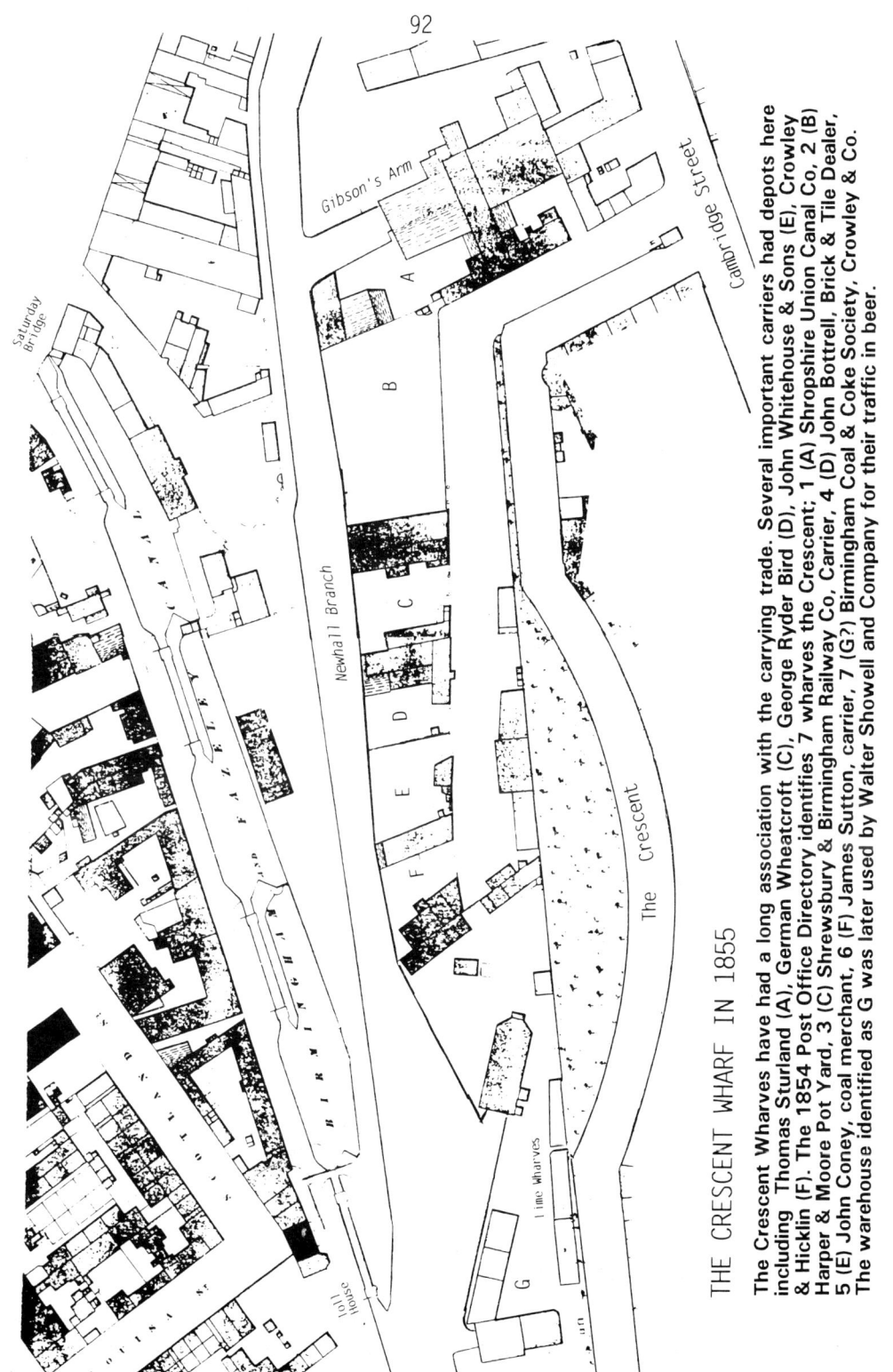

THE CRESCENT WHARF IN 1855

The Crescent Wharves have had a long association with the carrying trade. Several important carriers had depots here including Thomas Sturland (A), German Wheatcroft (C), George Ryder Bird (D), John Whitehouse & Sons (E), Crowley & Hicklin (F). The 1854 Post Office Directory identifies 7 wharves the Crescent; 1 (A) Shropshire Union Canal Co, 2 (B) Harper & Moore Pot Yard, 3 (C) Shrewsbury & Birmingham Railway Co, Carrier, 4 (D) John Bottrell, Brick & Tile Dealer, 5 (E) John Coney, coal merchant, 6 (F) James Sutton, carrier, 7 (G?) Birmingham Coal & Coke Society, Crowley & Co. The warehouse identified as G was later used by Walter Showell and Company for their traffic in beer.

Birmingham, to London. Judd took over the canal trade built up by Thomas Sherratt in October 1806 and also purchased Taylor's warehouse in December 1806 after Taylor was bankrupted. William Judd continued to carry by both canal and road. His road vehicles not only travelled to London, but also met the boats to carry goods to destinations away from the line of the canal. Waggons were also provided by carriers such as William Rudge to meet Judd's boats at Warwick and to forward goods onto places such as Stratford-upon-Avon, Moreton-in-Marsh, Cirencester and Tetbury. William Judd was made bankrupt in 1814 and his wharf passed to George Ryder Bird.

LONDON & BIRMINGHAM CARRYING CO LTD   WW

Registered in June 1890, this firm was established to take over the carrying concern of Joseph and Thomas Wiles, corn merchants of St Albans, Hertfordshire. The Grimsdale family, who were corn merchants at Uxbridge, became major shareholders in the business. In 1895 all but one of the shares were purchased by the Graham family of Birmingham. Thomas James Graham, wharfinger of Worcester Wharf, then became the majority shareholder and control of the company passed into his hands. At an extra-ordinary general meeting held at the office of Thomas Graham & Sons, Worcester Wharf 6th February 1899, the decision was taken to wind-up the London & Birmingham Carrying Co.

LONDON & STAFFORDSHIRE CARRYING CO   GC

Joshua and James Fellows were two of the partners which set up the London & Staffordshire Carrying Company in 1876. The firm was taken over by Fellows, Morton & Co in 1879.

NEEDHAM & WALKER   WW

Needham & Walker were Worcester carriers who commenced carrying on the Worcester & Birmingham Canal c1865 and continued until c1880 .

W. PARTRIDGE & CO   WW

William Partridge was a Worcester carrier who traded from Diglis Basin to Birmingham and Bristol. Partridge used the No 5 Worcester Wharf c1830-c1855.

PICKFORD AND CO   WW

Thomas and Matthew Pickford were Poynton carriers who established an extensive canal, rail and road carrying business. They first acquired a wharf in Birmingham, when they took over the Burton Boat Company's depot in Love Lane, Aston. In 1812 they transferred to a new wharf in Fazeley Street beside the

Warwick & Birmingham Canal which became their Birmingham depot. The completion of the Worcester and Birmingham Canal opened up a new trading route for them. At first, they leased a warehouse at Lowesmere, Worcester formerly used by Bird and Worthington. Then, about 1820, they rented the warehouse at No.4 Worcester Wharf beside Bridge Street and used this for landing goods sent along the Worcester and Birmingham line. When Pickford established themselves as railway carrier, their London trade and Fazeley Street depot was given to the Grand Junction Canal Company, but Worcester Wharf and the River Severn trade was retained until c1872.

PICTON & SONS   C

The Picton's were carriers at the Crescent from 1866-1941. They operated a service between Birmingham and Wolverhampton established by Charles Picton, a Wolverhampton boatman. It remained a family business and was finally controlled by Harold Keane Picton, who lived in Birmingham.

FREDERICK PIMM   WW

Frederick Pimm leased a portion of Worcester Wharf about 1840 and set up in business as a carrier and hay dealer. Pimm evidently traded on a small scale and only offered one service to Stratford-upon-Avon. Frederick and his family lived on the wharf and continued in business until c1855.

CHARLES PRATT JR   C

Charles Pratt used Crowley's Wharf to provide a service to Stratford upon Avon c1835-1845.

HENRY PRATT

Henry and Thomas Pratt were millers who took over Danks & Tyler's wharf in Wolverhampton and established a Fly boat service between Birmingham and Manchester about 1828. Henry was joined by James Shipton in 1831 who later took over the business.

MOSES ROBINSON   BS   BK

Moses Robinson joined Corbett in partnership about 1817 and traded from the Grand Junction Wharf, Broad Street, formerly Gibbins, Small & Co. They offered a service to Worcester for the Severn trade, and London by way of the Grand Junction Canal. By 1821 Corbett had left to trade from Aston Junction. Moses Robinson transferred the former Dudley Canal/ Timber Company basin during December 1823, which he renamed Regents Wharf. John Greaves bought this basin in 1823 and continued the allow Moses Robinson to use it. Robinson formed another partnership with William Partridge, but both were made bankrupt in March 1828.

J.ROWLANDS   WW

J. Rowlands operated a service to Henley in Arden, Stratford-upon-Avon c1815.

RICHARD RUDGE   FB

In 1816 Richard Rudge advertised a service to Derby and Shardlow three days a week. He had married, Elizabeth Swaine, widow of Thomas Swaine and operated the carrying concern set up by Thomas. The couple separated in September 1816 and Elizabeth took charge of the business and operated it under the title of the Late T.Swaine.

THOMAS RUSSELL & CO   C   OW

Thomas Russell started in the canal carrying trade as Russell, Hunter & Co. They had a warehouse and dock at the Old Wharf and are listed in Pyes 1791 directory as Coal and Limestone merchants. By June 1791 the firm had become simply Thomas Russell and Co which, at that time, was a partnership between Thomas Russell, Joseph Grundy and Thomas Grundy. They carried on business as coal dealers and general merchandise carriers between Birmingham and Stourport. In July 1791 Thomas Russell was given permission to erect a temporary warehouse on Farmers Wharf and became the first general carrier to trade from the Crescent. On 10th May 1794 Robert Skey, John Lee and Joseph Francis took over the firm but continued to trade as Thomas Russell & Co until 1797.

SEVERN & CANAL CARRYING CO   WW

This firm was established in 1873 and carried goods and merchandise to their depot in Bridge Street. At first they were known as the Severn & Canal Carrying , Shipping and Steam Towing Company Ltd, but this was shortened about 1891 to the Severn & Canal Carrying Co Ltd. From they were a subsidiary of the Sharpness New Docks & Gloucester & Birmingham Navigation Co. At various times the premises they possessed where enlarged and modified. The greatest expansion came in 1912 when they acquired the adjacent No 3 wharf from Moses Fraley. Their business taken over by the Docks & Inland Waterways Executive in October 1948.

SHAW & CO   FB

Shaw & Co advertised a service to Warwick, Banbury & Oxford in 1816 from Summer Row.

JOHN SHERRATT C

John Sherratt was a shopkeeper who was also a carrier. He traded from Judd's wharf to Hinckley and Nuneaton for a short period 1807-1813. John was made bankrupt January 1813. His one trading boat and a coal boat were offered for sale, 01 March 1813.

THOMAS SHERRATT C

Sherratt was a road carrier who started a fly boat service to Oxford in May 1792 after the Fazeley Canal had been linked to the Coventry Canal. Traffic was conveyed by canal to Oxford and then by Thames barges into London. Thomas first established a wharf at Aston Junction but moved to the Crescent in 1793, where he took the wharf next to Thomas Russell. By 1800, Sherratt was sending boats daily to the capital. Colcutts waggons met his boats at Oxford to carry merchandise forward to destinations as far as Southampton. William Judd also met his boats at Banbury to carry goods to Aylesbury, Buckingham, Uxbridge and Watford. Thomas Sherratt's fleet of boats eventually reached 14, but his financial position was not sound. A succession of bad winter and difficulties in getting sufficient return loading led to Sherratt's bankruptcy in June 1806. The business was taken over by William Judd, but Thomas Sherratt remained at the Crescent as Judd's agent.

SHIPTONS & CO BS C GC

The head of the Shipton family was Joseph who set up a timber merchants business at Charlotte Street, Birmingham, during 1807. He had a large family and several of his sons later joined him in the timber trade. Two of Joseph's sons, Maurice and James established a timber yard in Wolverhampton and later became merchandise carriers when they joined Henry Pratt in partnership. James Shipton took a particular interest in the carrying trade and leased a wharf in Birmingham from September 1831. It was known as the Albion Wharf and occupied part of the basin which faced Broad Street. For a brief time they traded as Shipton, Pratt & Co, but by 1834 had become Shiptons & Co. In 1839 Shipton took over George Ryder Bird's carrying business and operated both the Crescent and Broad St establishments. They now had become important canal carriers. Shiptons moved to Great Charles St in 1843 when James became a partner in the Swift Packet Company. Maurice Shipton left the firm about this time. With James Shipton now solely in charge of the carrying and timber business, the firm became simply Shipton & Co. In September 1849, Shipton & Co was taken over by the Duke of Bridgewater's Trustees, although the London trade was continued under Shipton's name until at least 1854. Shipton maintained a private basin in Great Charles Street for the use of the Swift Packet Company until 1851. James Shipton remained a timber merchant and stayed in this business until his death in February 1865.

SHROPSHIRE UNION RAILWAYS & CANAL CO   C

The Shropshire Union Railway and Canal Company entered the canal carrying trade in 1848 and built up an extensive business along the line of their canal from Ellesmere Port to Birmingham. During 1848 they acquired Thomas Sturland's wharf at the Crescent. Eventually four wharves at the Crescent, numbers 1,2,5 & 6, were used by them. They gave up the carrying trade in 1921 and their fleet was taken over by the London & North Western Railway Company.

SIMPSON, HYDE & NEW   BS

John Simpson offered a varied fly boat service to places as diverse as Leicester, Hull & Dudley from c1825-c1830.

R.S.SKEY   BS   C   WW

Robert Samuel Skey was a Stourport trader who had established a warehouse beside the canal at Broad Street by 1793. Skey was in partnership with Samuel Pemberton and Benjamin Stokes who owned the Coseley Ironworks. They traded together as Robert Samuel Skey & Co and were dealers in iron, paper and wine. The partnership was dissolved on 01 January 1794, but Skey formed another with John Lee Junior and Joseph Francis. As Skey, Lee and Francis, they took over the carrying trade of Thomas Russell. Their boats operated from both Broad St and the Crescent. This partnership was terminated in August 1797 when Robert Skey was left in charge of the carrying side of business. The Crescent wharf premises were given up about 1798, but Skey retained his wharf in Broad Street. This was situated beside a *private* cut which joined the Birmingham Canal. The premises included a house occupied by himself, a crane and a warehouse. During August 1797 Skey agreed to lease the BCN dock and dockyard opposite the Brasshouse and probably sub let it to George Ryder Bird. About 1805 Bird joined Skey in a partnership which lasted until June 1811 when Bird left to establish his own trade. Skey then had John Corbett as a partner and later Thomas Small. By 1816 he traded on his own again from the Worcester Wharf. Skey's financial position was not sound and to ease the burden, the Worcester Wharf warehouse was given up in 1819. Robert continued in business as a coal merchant and carrier at Stratford - upon- Avon with rented warehouses at

Stratford and Wootten Wawen. Eventually his debts overcame him and was made bankrupt in January 1821.

ROBERT SMALLWOOD   WW

Robert Smallwood offered a twice weekly service between Birmingham and Hereford which followed the Worcester & Birmingham Canal, the River Severn and the Gloucester & Hereford Canal. Robert was Birmingham born and lived at the Worcester Wharf with his wife. In trade directories he is described as a wharfinger and cider merchant and operated as such between 1830 and 1855.

SMITH & SONS   BS   GC

Smith & Son were early Burton-upon-Trent carriers who took goods along the Trent and Mersey to the port of Gainsborough. They used Worthington's Wharf in Great Charles Street.

SMITH & WILKINSON   GC

Benjamin Smith and George Wilkinson offered a service to Walsall (c1838-c1844) from their wharf at 159 Great Charles Street.

HENRY SOUTHAN   WW

Henry Southan was canal carrier who later extended his trade to carriage on the railways. Goods were taken by the Worcester and Birmingham Canal to Bristol and all parts of South Wales. Southan used No.3 Worcester Wharf c1825-c1855.

STAFFORDSHIRE & WORCESTER CANAL
CARRYING CO   WW

This carrying concern was established by the Staffordshire & Worcestershire Canal Company. By 1860 they had the use of one of the Worcester Wharves where William Smith was agent. The trade was later taken over by Joseph Fellows.

JAMES SUTTON & CO   C

Sutton and Co's were Derbyshire carriers who took over George Swaine's trade. Their boats operated from the Crescent during the 1850's and provided a service to Shardlow Derby, Gainsborough and Hull.

STRATFORD UPON AVON CANAL CARRYING CO WW

Took over the Ashwin & Co's trade c1860 and operated until mid 1860's. T.J Graham was their agent at Worcester Wharf.

THOMAS STURLAND C

Thomas Sturland had two carrying partnerships, first with Antwis and later with a gentleman named Tildasley. They were general canal carriers and dealt with goods for Liverpool, Manchester, London and Worcester. By 1845 Thomas Sturland traded on his own and advertised as both a canal and railway carrier. In 1848 his wharf (No.1, Crescent) and business was taken over by the Shropshire Union Railway & Canal Co.

GEORGE SWAINE & CO OW FB

There were three generations of the Swaine family who were canal carriers. George Swaine carried goods by road from Birmingham to the East Midlands before 1800, but is also known to have operated boats through the Dudley Tunnel as early as 1792. George was succeeded by his son Thomas who continued the road haulage business from a warehouse in New Street and also offered a canal service to Derby, Gainsborough, Hull and Nottingham. Thomas first used a warehouse at the Old Wharf, but later moved to Friday Bridge. An agreement also existed with John Dean of Oxford who carried goods on Swaine's behalf from Birmingham to Oxford. Thomas Swaine died during December 1813 and left his wife, Elizabeth, to carry on the business. Elizabeth Swaine had a short-lived partnership with Richard Rudge, which see, then operated the business herself for a number of years until her son, George, was of an age to take charge. George Swaine Junior continued as a railway and canal carrier until c1852.

THE BIRMINGHAM AND MIDLAND CANAL CARRYING COMPANY LTD WW

Incorporated during March 1965, this firm came into business as a general canal carrier. Their cargos were varied and included coal from the Leicestershire Coalfield to the Croxley Paper Mills near Watford, timber from Sharpness to Warwick and lubricating oil from Liverpool to Aldridge. No profit was obtained from these ventures and the firm accumulated a rapidly increasing debt. Between 1972 and 1975 they moved away from freight carrying into the passenger market and converted their fleet into trip and camping boats.

JOHN WALL & CO   BS

John Wall was West Bromwich carrier who traded on the canal by 1789. About 1793 Wall established a wharf beside Broad Street and opposite King Edwards Place. John was in partnership with Samuel Danks, for a time, and together they traded to Stourport. Danks commenced to operate on his own account from 1798, but continued to share the Broad Street Wharf with John Wall. Trade directories as late as 1801 still refer to John Wall & Co at Broad Street and make no mention of Samuel Danks until 1803. Wall ceased trading in 1803 and his business then passed to Henry Weeks. The Broad Street Wharf remained, however, in Danks' possession.

HENRY WEEKS   BS

Henry Weeks was a London carrier who traded along the line of the Grand Junction Canal. Weeks first used Adam, Southern & Company's wharf at Great Charles Street, but later moved to a wharf in Broad Street, opposite the Brasshouse, in 1803. Henry Weeks re-named the wharf, he used, the London & Stourport Wharf. In 1807, Weeks was made bankrupt and his property was disposed of between March and April that year. The business then passed to Thomas Dixon.

WHEATCROFT & SONS   FB   C

Nathaniel and German Wheatcroft were Cromford based carriers who first traded from Swaine's Wharf, but transferred to their own wharf at the Crescent in 1815. The Birmingham trade was later carried on under German Wheatcroft & Sons. They gave up their wharf (No 2 Crescent) c1844.

JOHN WHITEHOUSE & SONS   C

John Whitehouse started as a Dudley to London road carrier and later became a local canal carrier around Tipton. He is mentioned in trade directories from 1805, but had probably been a carrier for a number of years before this. John had several sons and three were later to assist him with the business. William Whitehouse was the eldest son. He and his brother, John, later became responsible for the management of the firm. John Whitehouse & Sons conveyed goods by canal to London and Worcester from their wharf at Tipton. A London fly boat service was also commenced which used Wheatcroft's wharf at the Crescent. New trading routes to Liverpool and Manchester were added subsequently. By 1821 Whitehouse & Sons rented their own wharf on the Crescent. Later John and William Whitehouse were assisted by their young brother Joseph. In 1848 the Whitehouse business and wharf (No 4 Crescent) was taken over by the Grand Junction Canal

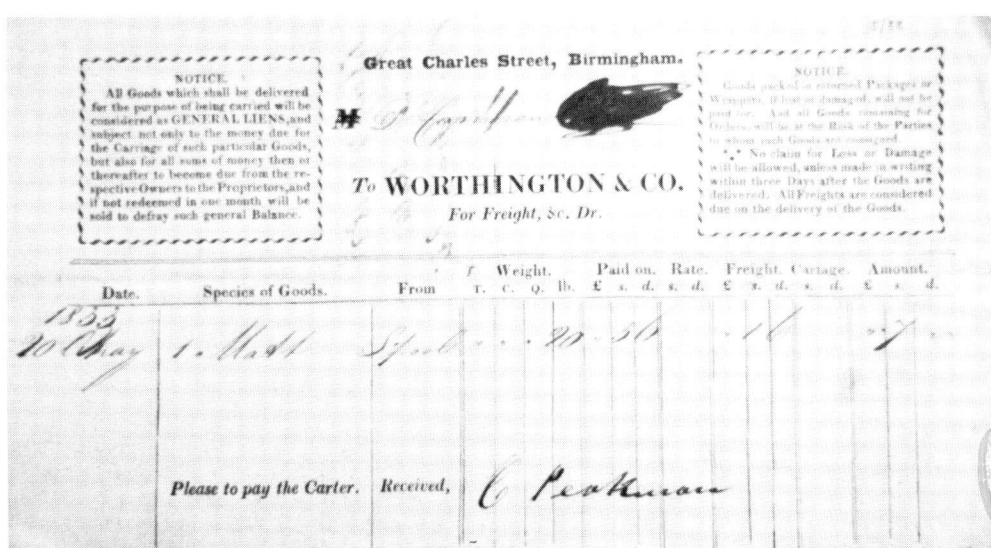

German Wheatcroft were Cromford carriers who took goods principally to the East Midlands. This invoice refers to a consignment of malt brought from Fazeley in September 1833.   *Courtesy Birmingham Library Archives (MS15,*

Worthington & Co carried goods from Liverpool and Manchester to Birmingham. Another consignment of malt was brought by them from Liverpool in May 1833
Courtesy Birmingham Library Archives (MS15)

Company. William died in 1850, but John continued in business as a coalmaster. John eventually retired and lived at Oakham, near Dudley until his death in 1869. Joseph Whitehouse became a iron merchant and established another canal carrying concern under his own name. He operated from a depot in High Street, West Bromwich. When Joseph died,in 1868, his canal trade was carried on by executors until 1886.

WORCESTER CARRYING CO   WW

Established by the Worcester and Birmingham Canal Co in 1848. The carrying trade was handed over to Joshua Fellows in 1868.

WORTHINGTON & CO   GC

Originally Worthington & Gilbert, Manchester traders. Their Birmingham trade passed to the Trustees of the Duke of Bridgewater in 1849.

SWIFT PACKETS.

Brm	Sth-wick.	Spon lane.	Ddly Port.	Tip-ton.	W'm ton.	W'm ton.	Tip-ton.	Ddly Port.	Spon lane.	Sth-wick	Brm
9 0	9 20	9 35	10 0	10 15	11 0	9 0	9 45	10 0	10 25	10 40	11 0
11 30	11 50	12 5	12 30	12 45	1 30	10 30	11 15	11 30	11 55	12 10	12 30
1 0	1 20	1 35	2 0	2 15	3 0	1 0	1 45	2 0	2 25	2 40	3 0
4 0	4 20	4 35	5 0	5 15	6 0	4 0	4 45	5 0	5 25	5 40	6 0
6 45	7 5	7 20	7 45	8 2	8 45	6 45	7 30	7 45	8 10	8 25	8 45

Packet Boats which provided a passenger service along the canal have already been mentioned in the text. These boats ran chiefly between Birmingham and Tipton, but were later extended to Wolverhampton. The Swift Packet boats were the last to operate from Birmingham. This service ceased when the Stour Valley Railway opened in 1852.

Former working boats can still be seen on the canal, some such as KESTREL are in privat ownership. KESTREL was a Fellows, Morton & Clayton Motor Boat, 218 in their fleet.

Thomas Clayton operated a fleet of boats from Oldbury chiefly for the carriage of tar and oil. They were named after rivers, a practice Thomas had inherited from his father, William. TOWY was a motor boat built in 1938.

Cambrian Wharf, February 1994. The MOUNTBATTEN (centre right) is moored near the top of Farmer's Bridge Locks. This is one of the few working boats left on canal. Her owner sells coal and diesel oil to fellow boatmen.

The Birmingham & Midland Canal Carrying Company Ltd started as a commercial venture and still carry the odd cargo. When the foundations for the new bridge across the canal opposite the ICC were excavated, No.6 was used to carry the spoil away.

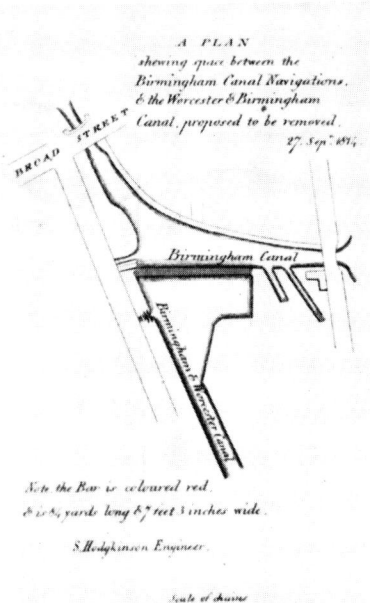

Right A plan of Worcester Bar in 1814. It would appear that it was once the intention to remove the entire Bar.
Courtesy Birmingham Archives

Below A sketch plan of the canal between Gas Street and Broad Street which shows a number of carriers basins;

Reference:

A   Gas Works Basin.

B   Coal Basin used by John Wynn and later by Greaves and Danks.

C   Boatyard used by G.R.Bird. Also probably used by H.Weeks.

D   Basin used by Danks, Shipton Skey and Wall.

E   Coal wharf, may have been used by Skey.

F   Old Wharf, used by Russell, Hunter & Co and Thomas Swain.

GAS STREET AND BROAD STREET

Broad Street (Islington)

Broad Street (Easy Row)

Birmingham Canal Navigations

Islington Basin

B

C

D

The Old Wharf

Worcester Bar

E

F

Netherton Basin

A

Gas Street

worcester and Birmingham Canal

Bridge Street

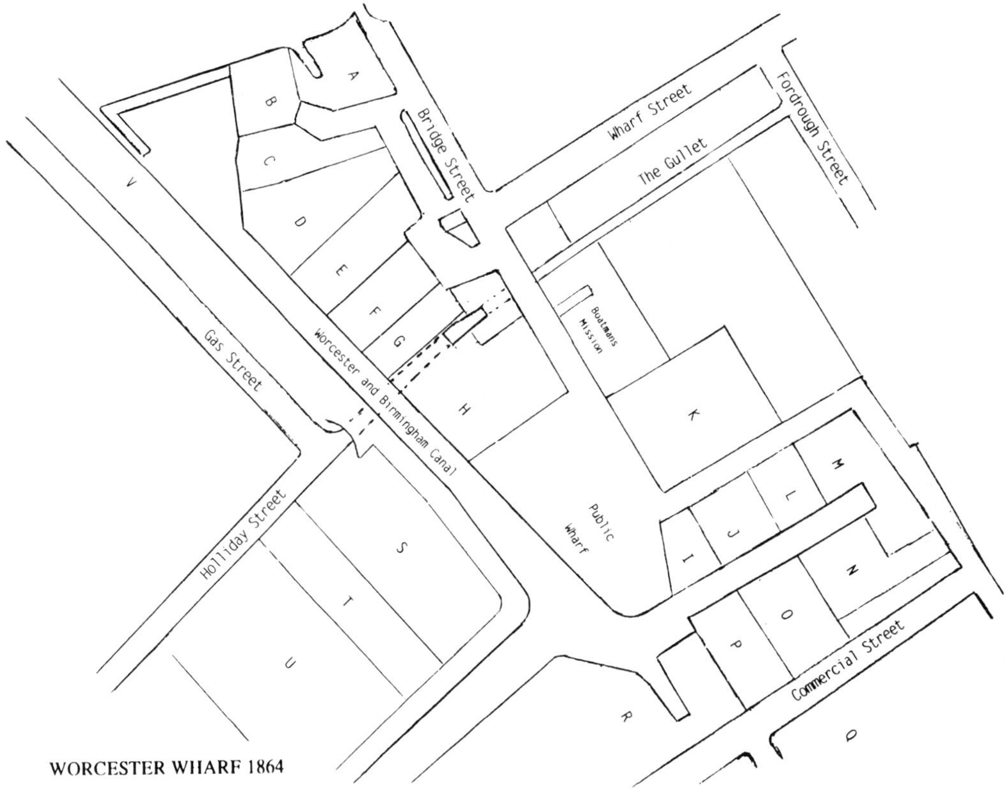

WORCESTER WHARF 1864

Worcester Wharf in 1864 was a complicated collection of waterside properties. A private road ran from Bridge Street to Commercial Street and served most of the wharves. In those days Bridge Street may not have dipped so steeply as it does today and the wharf road which joined it may have passed over the top of The Gullet.

Reference:

A	George Goodman	L	John Avins
B	Thomas Graham	M	J.B.Chirm
C	Vacant, formerly Sutton & Co	N	Thomas Short & Son
D	Pickford & Co, & James Fellows & Co	O	Vacant
		P	James Stevens
E	Vacant, formerly W.Partridge	Q	Site of old Canal Co Offices
F	Thomas Davis	R	James Stevens
G	Thomas Short & Son	S	Commissioner of Streets
H	John White	T	J & W Bennett
I	Robert Smallwood	U	Borough of Birmingham
J	Miles & Harford	V	New Canal Co. Offices
K	John Knight		

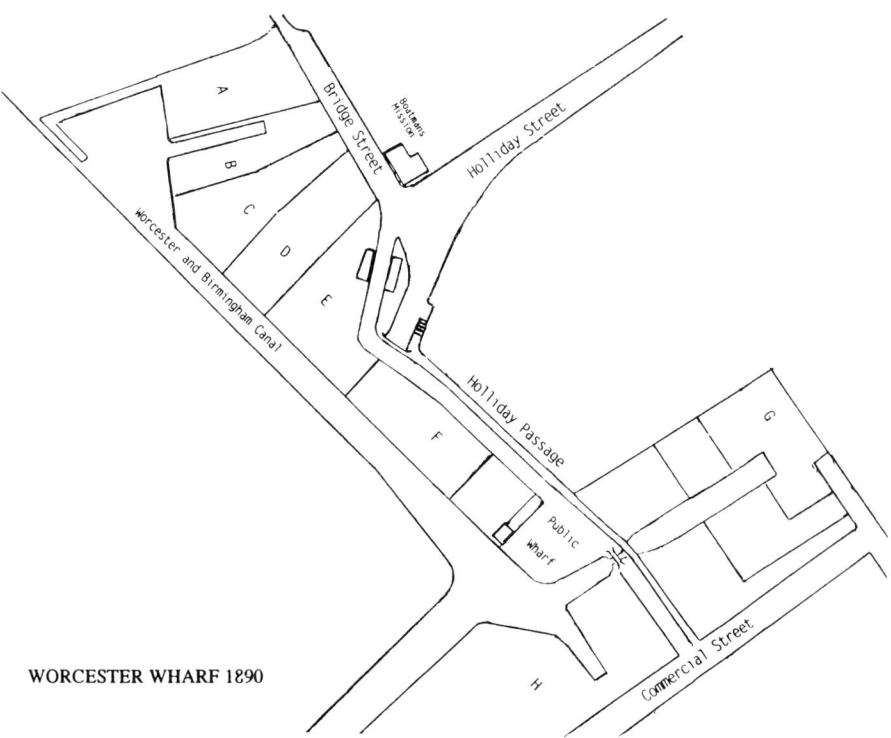

WORCESTER WHARF 1890

Worcester Wharf in 1890 had altered in many ways. The private road had been re-routed and now passed over the top of Holliday Street to reach the Public Wharf. A drawbridge also connected this wharf with another wharf road to Commercial Street. Several wharf properties were obliterated when the Midland Railway built their goods station. The original entrance from Blucher Street now only reached the timber wharves beside the top canal basin.

Reference;

A	Greaves Bull & Iakin Cement Wharf, Thomas Graham, Agent.
B	Fraley & Underhill, Marble Yard.
C	Severn Canal Carrying, Shipping & Steam Towing Co Ltd.
D	Timber Yard.
E	Timber Yard.
F	Timber Yard.
G	John Chirm's Timber Yard.
H	Timber Yard.

Several railway companies also carried goods on the canals. Within the midlands, the Great Western, Midland and London & North Western companies all had a share of the traffic. The Midland Railway even had a fleet of boats which operated from its depot at Great Bridge.

There were a few who, for a brief time, used wharves in the centre of Birmingham.

BIRMINGHAM, WOLVERHAMPTON & STOUR VALLEY RAILWAY

The Stour Valley Railway was built to provide a shorter route between Birmingham and Wolverhampton and also serve the extensive industry in between the two towns. From the start this railway was a subsidiary of the London & North Western Railway. Whilst the railway was under construction, Kingston Wharf became the property of the Stour Valley Company. It may have been used as a construction site for the tunnel which passed underneath, but also could have been used to ferry building materials to the contractors along the line.

NORTH STAFFORDSHIRE RAILWAY COMPANY.

The North Staffordshire took over James Shipton's carrying concern in 1847 and for two years provided a carrying service from Shipton's wharf in Great Charles Street. In 1849 they handed over this trade to the Duke of Bridgewater's Trustees. James Shipton remained their agent throughout.

SHREWSBURY & BIRMINGHAM RAILWAY COMPANY

In 1850 the Shrewsbury & Birmingham Railway was locked in a vicious battle with the London & North Western Railway over their right to use the Stour Valley Railway into Birmingham. The LNWR used both legal and physical tactics to block their every attempt. It was not until 1854 that S&BR trains were allowed to run into Birmingham. During these years the S&BR established a canal carrying depot at No.3 Crescent Wharf, presumably to carry their traffic to Wolverhampton where it would have been transhipped into railway waggons and taken to Shrewsbury or stations en route.

Sheepcote Street once had three tube works. Hudson Edmunds & Co Ltd were the last to survive. Their building still stands, although now out of use.

FORGOTTEN STREETS AND ROADS

Changing times and values have taken their toll on the streets of roads of Birmingham. Many have disappeared or have been re-named over the years. A list of those which once existed in the Gas Street area is given below:

Baskerville Passage

Was once a narrow passage way which crossed the Baskerville Canal basins. It ran from Baskerville Place to Easy Row.

Baskerville Place

A street which joined Broad Street: It is now part of Centenary Square.

Brasshouse Passage

A street which passed beside the Brasshouse and towards the canal. This street has been obliterated by the Waters Edge Development.

Crescent

Off Cambridge Street. The houses in this street were built in the shape of a crescent.

Crescent Street

From Kingston Row across Farmer's Bridge. This street was removed after Tindal Bridge was completed and Farmer's Bridge demolished.

Crown Street

See entry under Nelson Street. Later known as Sheepcote Street.

Easy Row

Easy Row took its name from Easy Hill where John Baskerville had his home. It ran from the top of Broad Street to Great Charles Street. This road is now part of Paradise Circus Queensway.

Fordrough Street

Also spelled as Fordrove Street. This street was removed when the Midland Railway built their Central Goods Station.

Islington

The old Hagley Turnpike from the BCN canal bridge to Five Ways was known as Islington. By 1839 it had become Broad Street (Islington). The original Broad Street which ran from Easy Row to the canal bridge became Broad Street (Easy Row). Separate street numbering sequences were used to distinguish the two parts, but eventually merged into one. The road then became simply Broad Street.

King Alfred's Place

From Cambridge Street to Broad Street. This street is now a pedestrian walk-way in front of the ICC

King Edward's Place

From Cambridge Street to Broad Street. This street disappeared when the International Convention Centre was built.

Mill Street

Later known as Grosvenor Street West, this street took it's name from the New Union Mill which faced the street.

Nelson Street

Sheepcote Lane originally ran from the Hagley Turnpike (Broad Street) to Summer Lane. During the early part of the nineteenth century. The part nearest Broad Street became Nelson Street, the central part, Crown Street and the remainder retained the name Sheepcote Lane. Nelson Street ran from Broad Street to the Old Birmingham Canal Bridge. It was a name that appears only a few maps and Sheepcote Street soon replaced it.

Nile Street

From Sheepcote Street to the canal. Nile Street appears in trade directories from 1845 and originally served brick wharves beside the canal. Later it served the Albion Tube Works.

Norfolk Street

Named after the county. All trace of this street was removed when the Midland Railway built their Central Goods Station.

Oozells Street

This street ran from Broad Street to the coal wharves on the Old Birmingham Canal. It has been closed to allow for the development of Brindley Place. The *Oozells* was originally a farm which stood near this road. It gave its name to both the street and this part of the Colmore Family Estate.

Oozells Street North

Part of Oozells Street was also known by this title.

St Martins Place

This road ran from St Martins Row to Broad Street and was removed when the ICC was built.

St Martins Row

St Martins Row ran from Cambridge Street to join St Martins Place. This street was removed when the ICC was made.

St Peters Row

This Row ran from Broad Street to St Martins Row. Odd pieces still remain, but most was removed when the ICC was made.

Tindal Street

Renamed Browning Street

Tindal Row

Perhaps another name for Kingston Row. It may also have been known as Crescent West.

Wharf Street

Part of this street was removed when the Central Goods Station was built, the rest became Holliday Street.

CHRONOLOGY

1768	8 Geo III c 38, 24/02/1768, Birmingham Canal Act
1772	Birmingham Canal completed
1773	New BCN offices built opposite their wharf in Suffolk Street.
1774	Partnership established between Matthew Boulton and James Watt.
1775	Death of John Baskerville, printer.
1777	Hugh Henshall leases wharf land in Great Charles Street from Charles Colmore.
1780	Birmingham Metal Company formed. The Brasshouse is established in Broad Street.
1783	23 Geo III c 92, 24/06/1783, Birmingham & Fazeley Canal Act
	St Peters Roman Catholic Church established on Easy Hill.
1791	Thomas Russell establishes a carriers wharf at the Crescent.
1792	10/06/1792, Worcester & Birmingham Canal Act.
1793	Birmingham Coal Company established.
1814	Articles of Birmingham Brewery made 22/03/1814
	New Union Mill established.
1815	55 Geo III c 40, 12/05/1815, Act to establish Bar Lock
1816	Birmingham Timber Company cease trading.
1817	John Gostling builds first gasworks in Birmingham.
1818	Central streets in Birmingham lighted with gas.
1819	Birmingham Gas Light & Coke Company formed.
1850	The Gas Works in Gas Street cease production.
1851	Bingley Hall built.
1862	Church of the Messiah opened in Broad Street.
1864	Worcester & Birmingham Canal Company transfer offices to 6 Gas Street.
1874	7/1874, Gloucester & Berkeley Canal acquire Worcester & Birmingham Canal.
1876	Granville Street Station opens.
1885	Granville Street Station closes.
	The Midland Railway complete their Central goods station.
	New aqueduct over Holliday Street completed.
1926	16/17 Geo 5 16/06/1926 Act for Abandonment of Old Wharf
1940	Baskerville House built
1948	1/1/1948 BCN and Sharpness Company taken over by British Transport Commission.
1949	Fellows Morton & Clayton cease trading
1968	Rail House, later Quayside Tower, opened.
1971	New Repertory Theatre opens.
1986	31/10/1986 Jacques Delors lays foundation stone for Convention Centre.
1991	International Convention Centre opened by the Queen 12/06/1991. National Indoor Arena completed.
1993	November, the last hire boat leaves Sherborne Street Wharf.
1994	Waters Edge Development opened.

BIBLIOGRAPHY

A number of sources have been drawn on, particularly those in Birmingham Library and Archives which include:

Aris's Gazette.
Birmingham Botanical Gardens papers MS15.
Birmingham Canal Navigations Documents MS86.
Birmingham Corporation Building Plans.
Birmingham Corporation Public Works Department Minutes.
Birmingham Gas, Light & Coke Company Minute Books.
Birmingham Journal.
Birmingham Levy and Rate Books.
Birmingham Timber Company Documents MS4.
Boulton & Watt Collection.
Matthew Boulton Papers.
Cadbury Collection MS466.
Caddick & Yates Documents.
Calender & Deeds of the Colmore Estate.
Fellows Morton & Clayton Papers MS454.
Galton Family Papers.
Gooch Estate Deeds.
King Edward VI School, plans & property 478632-478673.
Lee, Crowder Deposit.
The Robins Collection MS275.
Robbins and Gillan Papers MS4.
Surveyors Office- Government Inquiry Plans & Documents.
Trade Directories, Birmingham, various dates 1766-1966.
Winfield Ltd., Papers MS322.

Other Sources include:

Public Records Office, Kew,
       Birmingham Canal Navigations, Minute Books RAIL 810.
       Sharpness New Docks & Gloucester & Birmingham Navigation Company Records. RAIL 864
       Worcester & Birmingham Canal, Minute Books RAIL 886.

Stafford Record Office
       Birmingham Canal Navigations Papers.
       Earl of Dartmouth Papers.
       Shipton Family Papers. D660 22-25.

Grateful thanks are also given to:

The Birmingham Library Staff
The Birmingham & Midland Carrying Company Ltd.
The BCN Society
Cadburys Ltd
Steve Crook
Tom Foxon
Alan Faulkner
Stanley Holland
John Miller
Ian Minter
Martin O'Keefe
The Railway Canal & Historical Society
Regional Railways
Patrick Thorn
Chris & Fiona Upton

·········· ✱ ··········

A question for the observant. The firm of Handyside were well known victorian engineers. A structure on the trail bears their manufacturers plate. Where is this structure and what is the date on the plate?